Endorsements

"Judy Russell writes from a deep and intimate relationship with God, who invites us all to His table of grace. Having lingered long, and with much laughter, at Judy's long table with her family, I found the same joy, the same hospitality, the same welcoming Jesus on these pages. Judy's heartwarming stories and her winsome wisdom is a feast for the soul!"
 —Ann Voskamp, author the New York Times Bestsellers, The Broken Way and One Thousand Gifts

"It has been my joy to know Judy and Bob Russell for over a couple of decades. It has been my greater joy to sit at their table. I am a beneficiary of Judy's kind hospitality. We are grateful that she has gone to the time and effort to compile these invaluable stories and memories. They will be treasured for generations to come."
 —Max Lucado, pastor and bestselling author

"The root of *hospitality* is *hospital*, and that is exactly what being a guest in Judy Russell's home is—a healing experience for mind, body, and spirit. As a physician, friend, and appreciative guest, I can attest that fellowship around the Russell's table offers medicine our world desperately needs."
 —Matthew Sleeth, MD, executive director of Blessed Earth and author of *Hope Always: How to Be a Force for Life in a Culture of Suicide*

"Having experienced Judy Russell's grace-filled hospitality countless times, I can't think of anyone more qualified to write this book. *Elbows on the Table* reveals that the core of all hospitality lies not in striving for perfection—but in expressing God's love to all who sit around our tables. Or as Judy puts it, *people over perfect*. This book is well-written, funny, touching, and full of practical wisdom. Buy it by the case and distribute it widely!"
 —Rebecca Manley Pippert, author of *Stay Salt* and *Out of the Salt Shaker*

"Romans 12:13 entreats us to "practice hospitality." With her trademark humility, honesty, and humor, Judy shares decades of practical wisdom on how to be a thoughtful and loving host. *Elbows on the Table* is a must-read for anyone seeking to transform their home into a place of shalom."

—Nancy Sleeth, managing director of Blessed Earth and author of *Almost Amish: One Woman's Quest for a Slower, Simpler, More Sustainable Life*

"Judy's book is a must read for anyone intimidated by the idea of hospitality. It is charming and inspirational. Wisdom, humor and charm fill this book and will have you throwing open your doors to practice the art of hospitality. I highly recommend it."

—Angela Correll, Co-Founder, Wilderness Road Hospitality, Author of the *May Hollow Trilogy*

"I'm blessed to call Judy a dear friend and mentor. Her unshakable dedication to her husband Bob during the many decades of his ministry became her own as well, not only regarding Southeast Christian Church, but also with her Sweet Spirit Singers, women's ministry, and The Living Word Bookstore—all the while being a mother, grandmother, and devoted friend.

"A fellow Butter Babe—we Babes call Judy "Butter Superior" as we all know she's *the* Queen of Hospitality—so who better to write a book on it? Judy's taught me and many others how to hunt and gather. This is one of dozens of ideas on hospitality you'll gain from reading this book, plus, don't miss the recipes! Tears of laughter and joy just may splash onto your book.

"Getting a peek into the Russell's lives around their dinner table is an added bonus. *Elbows on the Table* will be an invaluable resource you'll return to time and time again. The extra elements on faith and prayer woven throughout Judy's life are heartwarming, inspirational, and an encouragement to us all to pray about *everything*."

—Elizabeth Hoagland, author of *Let's Be Friends—What My Sister-Friends Taught Me About Faith, Food, and Fun*

ELBOWS
on the
TABLE

Simple Ways to Make Gathering Better

Judy Russell

WESTBOW
PRESS
A DIVISION OF THOMAS NELSON
& ZONDERVAN

[Handwritten inscription: Enjoy Gathering 1st 4:9 Judy Russell]

WestBow Press books may be ordered through booksellers or by contacting:

WestBow Press
A Division of Thomas Nelson & Zondervan
1663 Liberty Drive
Bloomington, IN 47403
www.westbowpress.com
844-714-3454

Because of the dynamic nature of the Internet, any web addresses or links contained in this book may have changed since publication and may no longer be valid. The views expressed in this work are solely those of the author and do not necessarily reflect the views of the publisher, and the publisher hereby disclaims any responsibility for them.

Managing Editor: Patt Alderdice Senseman
Cover Design: Karis Pratt
Photographer: Nick Bonura
Illustrations: Martha Brammer

ISBN: 978-1-6642-7462-4 (sc)
ISBN: 978-1-6642-7461-7 (e)

Print information available on the last page.

WestBow Press rev. date: 10/04/2022

Dedication

Thank you to my sweet husband, Bob, who has patiently read these pages many times and encouraged me not to quit.

To my son Rusty and his family: thank you for waiting with patience, teasing and encouraging me to continue, and loving me.

And to my son Phil and his family, who have lived a lifetime in the shadow of parents and grandparents and yet encouraged and always loved me.

Thank you, each one. I love you all dearly.

In Honor of Debbie DePorter

This book is in honor of my friend, Debbie DePorter, who was a gal that said yes to entertaining and hosting guests often. Her husband Eugene, is our churches' pastor for new church plants throughout America. Debbie and Eugene hosted ministers and missionaries that came to visit our church for years.

They hosted small groups, class parties, and Bible studies. People loved being in their home, and Debbie loved people.

Sadly, Debbie battled cancer. Yet she still worked and served, loving on folks and opening her door often.

Debbie is home with Jesus today. I'm sure she is helping to greet and host people coming through the gates of Heaven. I look forward to sharing with her again. I miss you, Debbie.

A Tribute to Preachers Wives

I never wanted to marry a preacher. Growing up across the street from our small church and watching how some church members treated the preacher, I didn't want that for my life. But I fell in love with a man called to preach. When he asked me to marry him, I said yes.

Here I am, 57 years later, writing about hospitality. And guests are coming for dinner in three hours. Once again, I said yes.

To be honest, we've had a wonderful life. In my wildest dreams, I never would imagine all the places we've traveled and the people we've met. Hundreds of preachers, missionaries, college kids, authors, politicians, sports figures and special people that walked through our front door. The hundreds of people who graced us by putting their elbows on our table. I'm glad I said yes to being a preacher's wife.

But it's not always been easy. There have been countless hours of serving with my husband, caring for our children and volunteering at the church. Most people don't have a clue what preacher's wives and their families do. You seldom hear a thank you be spoken. It's easy to get frustrated when you are expected to do everything.

We know we're supposed to be supportive and respectful of our husband but sometimes it's difficult.

Pastor's wives, you are special women. There are times you said yes to a specific task, because years ago you said yes to the man beside you. God chose you and equipped you to serve along with your husband.

Thank you for continuing to serve, even though it can be difficult enduring the tough times of ministry. Thank you for saying yes to loving your husband and thank you for respecting him, regardless of the circumstances.

Dear One, thank you for saying yes to God and following through with His plan.

I will meet you in the morning, my friend, *Just Inside the Eastern Gate.**

*Albert E. Brumley
https://hymnary.org/text/i_will_meet_you_in_the_morning_just_insi#authority_media_audio

Contents

Introduction

YES, ELBOWS ON THE TABLE

I've thought back over life-changing times when I said yes. Several stand out to me.

As a fifth grader, deep water terrified me, but I said yes to accepting Jesus as my Lord and Savior, and being baptized by immersion.

When I was an eighth-grader, they asked me to be the pianist at our church for worship services. I said yes.

As a junior in high school, they asked me to be the ways and mean's chairperson for our class and raise money for our junior trip. I said yes, and we went to Washington DC.

Then I was asked to try out for the senior play. I said yes and got the supporting actress role. In college they asked me to join a girls' trio. I said yes, and we traveled representing the school.

It's not the cooking that makes a meal, but the company.

Our trio was singing at a yearly conference when my husband Bob spotted me. He asked me for a date, and I said yes. That yes led to a big life-changing yes when he asked me to marry him. And I was never planning to marry a preacher. Ha! God was preparing me for a ministry role all along and is still grooming me today.

In my wildest dreams, I never imagined the people we would meet, the places we would go and the experiences we've had.

Hundreds of preachers, friends. and family have graced our home over the years. Foreign missionaries, college students, noted authors, sports figures, and politicians have come through our front door. Even a homeless man—twice! I am overwhelmed with how many blessed us and put their elbows on our dining room table. I said yes and I am forever amazed!

When you are having guests in your home, sometimes you haven't finished straightening things. We may have piled our coffee table with magazines and papers. And that's okay; people are more important. Enjoy the people gathered in your home. It's always people over perfection.

We have a lifetime of great memories with people who have put their elbows on our table. It's not about the food, successes, or disasters, but the people.

When someone puts their elbows on your dinner table, it shows they are comfortable. They are leaning in and engaged in conversation. They are enjoying the time together. Today's relaxed etiquette allows for elbows on the table when you and your guests are not eating.

You may ask, "Have you used the ideas in this book?" You bet I have! I have gathered entertaining and hospitality ideas my whole life. It started with more formal dining and has gradually changed over the years to our style today: casual, warm, and comfortable.

I've learned to forgo fresh flowers on the dinner table. Use plastic plates and cups for more casual gatherings. In a pinch? Grab a can of soup, and fix a grilled cheese sandwich. Stock up on cold cuts. Short on ice? Skimp on ice cubes or borrow from your neighbor. And get to know the best caterer in your city.

I've tucked in a few surprises—favorite family recipes, tips for parties, table settings, and more.

My prayer is you will find inspiration and encouragement. Take notes in the margins and highlight the words. Share ideas you have discovered. And keep gathering new ideas. As a result, I hope you say yes to elbows on your table.

A small plaque in our kitchen states,

"It's not the cooking that makes a meal, but the company."

CHAPTER 1

People Over Perfect

> "He must be hospitable, one who loves what is good,
> who is self-controlled, upright, holy, and disciplined."
>
> *Titus 1:8, NIV*

MUST EVERYTHING BE perfect for guests? Yes, ma'am, that was me. I remember a sultry, humid Sunday in Kentucky when I was overwhelmed and felt like nothing could be perfect anymore. Ever.

A Life-Changing Afternoon

After multiple worship services, Bob and I often took a Sunday afternoon nap. But neither of us rested on that specific Sunday.

Instead, I toured model homes looking for decorating ideas, as there were no Pinterest boards in 1995. Bob was in a meeting at the church where he was the senior pastor.

Once home, I repotted a Peace Lily, plopped in my armchair, propped my feet up, and flipped on the TV. I awakened when the remote fell from my hand. My left arm and leg tingled. I stood up and stumbled across the carpet. I knew something was not right, and desperate for help, I dialed 911.

I couldn't get the operator to understand me.

"Never mind, I'm going to my neighbor's." I hung up the phone, not realizing I had been slurring my words.

I discovered a precious fact—I am not indispensable, and my home's not ideal.

I staggered across our yard to the neighbor's steps. 'Oh, Lord, they have to be here,' I thought as I rang the doorbell and steadied myself against the wall. Joy opened the door and looked at my twisted face. She seized my arm and walked me into her front hall, motioning for me to sit on the floor. Joy began asking questions, and I tried explaining as she checked my blood pressure and called EMS.

"Where's Bob?" Joy asked.

"He's at a church meeting."

Her husband Phil darted out to find him.

We heard the wailing sirens as the EMS driver sped onto our street. First responders arrived and asked questions while they rushed me to the hospital emergency room.

I suffered a stroke that affected my left side, making it hard to walk. My left hand was weak, and I lost the feeling in my fingers. Therapy, medications, and a slower-paced lifestyle sent me down a new road.

This road was marked with panic when my heart went out of rhythm. For several years, I was scared when alone, as anxiety reigned. Satan tricked me to think the worst, even though I trusted in God's care and protection. I worked hard to concentrate on positive thinking.

My dear husband Bob was a great encourager and prayer warrior. He took me to countless doctor appointments and tests. He ran errands, picked up prescriptions and groceries, and endured my watching Martha Stewart and HGTV.

Friends, our two sons, and sweet daughters-in-law took turns staying with me. People took me to lunch, and friends brought meals and cooked at my house. People came and cleaned and did our laundry. My hairdresser came to my house to fix my hair. I am forever grateful.

My life as a multi-tasker changed as my energy level plummeted. I didn't want to read, watch much TV, make my bed, or do laundry. I was happier staying home than going out, and my favorite thing was seeing my family—especially our baby grandson.

Six months after my stroke and an allergic reaction to the anti-seizure medication, I was doing somewhat better. Christmas was only a few weeks away. I love Christmas. But I didn't care if the house got decorated or the tree trimmed. I wasn't capable of decorating anymore. How blessed I am with loving friends who came to help and finish decorating.

The doctors released me to drive, but I never ventured far. Exhaustion overtook me, and I needed to rest. A long 18 months passed before I was back to my new normal. Everything was different, and our home didn't need to be perfect. I planned to-do lists and when things got checked off, yay for me! If not, I moved the items to the next day's page.

I discovered a precious fact—I am not indispensable, and my home's not ideal.

My attempts at being a good preacher's wife, mother, grandmother, sister, and friend are not perfect. Only my Lord and Savior Jesus Christ is the Perfect One.

Yes, I've always longed for tasks done well. But after my stroke, I recognized my attempts may not be as I expected anymore. The world is not perfect. And I am far from perfect.

We have a small plaque in our kitchen that reads, 'It's not the cooking that makes a meal, but the company.' Enjoy your imperfect home and love the people who walk through your door.

Tuna Casserole for Our Guest

Our first wedding anniversary in 1966 was spent moving to Louisville, Kentucky. Bob accepted the position of pastor at Southeast Christian Church, a small church full of potential. We prayed for wisdom and discernment and although excited, scared, and unsure, we said yes. God has blessed that decision ever since.

As we settled into our new apartment, Bob wanted to invite our youth pastor over for lunch. "He will be our first guest to eat here."

I decided on tuna casserole[1] and served sides of fresh peas and applesauce.

As soon as I took my first bite of casserole, I realized my mistake. Oh, no! How stupid of me.

Embarrassed and humiliated, I admitted, "I'm so sorry, but I forgot to put the tuna in the casserole. I can add the tuna and put it back in the oven."

Both guys said no. They liked the cheesy filling and continued eating. My salvation? I always added lots of yummy cheese.

Our Parents Away from Home

We were young Bible college students, dating and falling in love. Bob was a youth pastor in Cincinnati, and we were hungry and always broke on Sunday nights.

As I sat through a church service one Sunday night, I glanced across the aisle, wondering if the Roots might invite us to their house for something to eat. They often invited us for peanut butter and banana sandwiches after church. If we were lucky, and if their budget allowed, they might have homemade chili with beans.

One evening Mrs. Root appeared stressed.

She said, "Judy, the only thing I have for sandwiches tonight is bread and sandwich spread. But you and Bob are more than welcome to come and join us."

"It's okay, I grew up on sandwiches made with sandwich spread. It is fine with us," I responded, thinking that is better than Bob and I spending our last dollar and splitting a plain McDonald's hamburger.

The Roots were lovely people. Mr. Root was an author and editor at a Christian publishing company. Mrs. Root, a homemaker.

We would sit around their tiny kitchen table, talk, and laugh about church, school, writing, basketball, family, and friends. Time spent talking with them was special as they asked questions, listened, and advised. They were our away-from-home parents.

CHAPTER 2

1000 and Counting

"I know the plans I have for you," declares the
Lord, "plans to prosper you and not to harm
you, plans to give you hope and a future."

Jeremiah 29:11, NIV

I WALKED PAST the dining room window just in time to get a
glimpse of a guy doing cartwheels across our front lawn. 'Who
is that?', I wondered. The van had arrived with my husband
Bob's mentoring retreat attendees. Each month, the eight attendees had dinner at our home.

I hurried to open the door. Two guys were laughing at their friend as he skipped and danced through our yard.

"He is so excited to be at Bob Russell's house he is doing cartwheels across your yard," one guy said. Now that puts the pressure on a host and hostess!

"Come on in," I said, swinging open the door and greeting our visitors. I can hear our neighbors thinking now, 'Dinner guests just arrived at the Russell's. This time they are doing acrobatic routines on their front lawn.'

Mentoring Ministers

After Bob retired, he wanted to start a mentoring program for preachers and call it "A Time of Refreshing."[2] His aim was to do a retreat for three and a half days with three goals: teach them, encourage them, and pamper them. Since September 2006, we've hosted over 1.000 different preachers at a Wednesday night dinner in our home. They minister to churches of 50-10,000 people and come from different states, countries, backgrounds, ethnic groups, and are of varying ages. What a blessing to meet and talk with faithful servants of God.

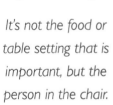

It's not the food or table setting that is important, but the person in the chair.

On Tuesday evening we take the retreat attendees to Ruth's Chris Steakhouse. It may be their first time to eat at a 4-star restaurant with dinnerware, starched linen napkins, and tablecloths. The Ruth's Chris in Louisville is on the top floor of a high-rise building with a 360-degree view of the city. The servers offer recommendations, inviting the guys to try various things. They laugh with them and tease, helping them to feel comfortable.

What a treat to watch them try lobster or choose a mammoth steak and take a picture to send home. The restaurant staff serve them an amazing meal with perfect service. An unforgettable evening!

On Wednesday night at the Russell's, reality returns when grilled chicken breasts, mashed potatoes and gravy, seasonal vegetables, Caesar salad, and bread is served buffet style. Or it might be juicy pork barbecue with mac and cheese, slaw and chips. We top the dinner off with a slice of warm Kern's Kitchen Derby pie and Graeter's ice cream.

I serve everything on colorful plastic plates, silverware, cups, and dessert plates. I lay large, brightly colored paper napkins at each place setting before guests arrive. Remember, it's not the food or table setting that is important, but the person in the chair.

LED candles are on throughout the house and fresh flowers are on the table. The large "Welcome to the Russell's" chalkboard sign greets retreat attendees as they walk up the step to our home. A seasonal wreath hangs on the front door. I have turned table lamps and chandeliers on to make our home more inviting. We want our guests to understand that fancy china and gourmet meals are unnecessary to have an enjoyable evening. Use those another time.

After we serve dessert, Bob asks each preacher to show us a picture of his wife and tell what he admires and appreciates about her. Sometimes it becomes an emotional evening. Seldom do guys stop and tell others why they love their wives. But they do that night. And often, I will bring out a box of tissues. Yes, guys weep too.

We try to make it a relaxed evening. Sometimes they will gather around the piano and sing. How amazing to hear men's voices harmonize old anthems and hymns and contemporary songs written from the scriptures.

Sometimes there might be a surprise. One guy brought an engagement ring he was planning to give his girlfriend the next night when she picked him up at the airport. He passed it around for us to see, explaining how they met and what he admired about her.

That fun evening in our home is one of sharing and visiting together—a simple dinner and great conversation.

At the mentoring retreat's closing session, Bob will ask, "What was your greatest takeaway?"

Their answer is often, "Going to the Russell's for dinner."

I am humbled by their words. They appreciate the opportunity of being in our home and placing their elbows on our table. Was it memorable? Yes, but nothing fancy.

One Memorable Dinner Guest

I recall an evening when a group flew in from Virginia. They were young preachers just out of college. John, who brought them, called me and said, "One guy has a birthday on Wednesday. Could you pick up a small cake so we can surprise him and celebrate?"

"Sure. What is his name?"

"His name is Nabeel."

I placed the decorated cake in front of our guest. The baker had written "Happy Birthday Nabeel," on the top and candles glowing made a handsome presentation. One candle played "Happy Birthday." Everyone erupted singing, "Happy Birthday to you". Tears filled Nabeel's eyes as he said words that broke my heart.

"I've never had a birthday cake. I've never had a party."

Those words may have meant nothing to the others. But making something special for this young preacher blessed me. It took extra time and effort to get a cake. I could have said no. But I'm so thankful God orchestrated that evening.

Nabeel Qureshi, a Pakistani-American Christian apologist, converted to Christianity from Ahmadiyya while in college.

Several years later, he moved to London and continued his

biblical studies at Oxford University. His love for the Bible and apologetics paved the road to becoming a sought-after speaker on college campuses, at churches, and in debates across the country.

Not only was Nabeel a thought-provoking speaker, but his first book, *Seeking Allah, Finding Jesus*[3], was on the New York Times Best Seller list in September 2015.

The first time in awards history, Nabeel received the Christian Book Award for the categories of both Best New Author and Best Non-Fiction in 2015. Nabeel's book, *No God but One: Allah or Jesus?*[4] was also a New York Times bestseller in 2016.

Over the years, Nabeel would call and say, "I'm coming through Louisville to speak. Is it okay to stay at your house?" Our door was always open for Nabeel and his wife to stay.

And then we got a disheartening word from him. He was battling a serious stomach cancer. Nabeel died a year later.

I remember going the extra mile to get a cake and celebrate a young man's birthday we didn't even know. It was an evening to remember.

Since then, I have seen how God uses Nabeel Qureshi's messages, debates, and interviews to spread the gospel. For certain, God is using him mightily.

We miss you, Nabeel.

CHAPTER 3

Simplest Hospitality: It's Not Always About Food

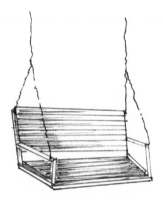

"Keep on loving one another as brothers and sisters. Do not forget to show hospitality to strangers, for by so doing some people have shown hospitality to angels without knowing it."

Hebrews 13:1, 2, NIV

TO ENTERTAIN MEANS it's about me, my house, my food, my table, showing off my Pinterest-perfect abode. Hospitality, however, is about showing people love. It's about opening your home, your heart, your lives, and showing them the love of God in action, word, and deed.

Hospitality is a command, not a choice.

Scripture commands us to show hospitality.

Do you remember a time experiencing hospitality that left a lasting impression on you—perhaps not at that moment, but later?

Grandparent Love

When I was about three years old, we moved into my grandparent's house. A door in our kitchen led to my grandparent's side of the house. Many nights we knocked on their door and waited to hear, "It's open". They knew we would come over for some grandma and grandpa time. They had already unlocked the door.

My grandmother covered the gigantic round kitchen table with a white cloth. There were dishes of food left over from the evening meal, along with newspapers and books lying on the table under the cloth. The cloth protected the food from flies or whatever else might fly around.

As a preschooler, I enjoyed listening to adult conversations while I nibbled leftovers from their gigantic round table.

I often crawled up on my grandfather's lap to snuggle a bit. He would pour steaming hot coffee into a deep saucer and add a spoonful of sugar and stir until the sugar disappeared.

Then he added pure cream, stirring it into the black coffee and melted sugar. As if by magic, it turned a creamy color.

I remember him lifting his spoon to my mouth to savor that sweet and yummy treat. Ah, my very first Cappuccino, 78 years ago. Although today, I'm not a coffee drinker. But if you added enough cream and sugar, maybe I could be. My grandfather was showing me hospitality as he shared from his saucer full of love.

My grandmother showed hospitality when she offered to

make me a sugar sandwich. I loved that old Irish treat. People used to fix this snack when they were low on money. My grandmother grew up eating sugar sandwiches.

She would give me a squeeze as I walked in her kitchen, lean down and whisper, rolling her eyes, "You want a sugar sandwich?" Ah, she knew the answer to the question. Shh, our little secret.

My grandmother prepared the sugar sandwich with a slice of fresh-baked bread and a hunk of churned butter. In those days, it was not a simple task to churn butter or bake the bread. There were no additives or preservatives, either. I can close my eyes and imagine the bread baking in her oven.

Hospitality is a command, not a choice.

She pulled open the drawer of a big pie safe and took out a loaf of homemade bread wrapped in a tea towel. As she placed the bread on the table and unwrapped the towel to expose a golden-crusted loaf of bread, I couldn't stand still. She cut off two thin pieces, preparing to slather some homemade butter on each slice.

Then my grandmother pulled the hem of her dress up and climbed down creepy and treacherous steps to the cellar. It was years before I ventured down those steps. Too scary.

They kept things in the cellar to stay cool and fresh. This was refrigeration for foods and jars of canned goods. Perfect for keeping milk and homemade ice cream and churned butter.

When she came back up the steps, she was carrying a bowl of butter.

My grandmother laid the two pieces of sliced bread on a plate, buttering each one. She took a teaspoon of coarse white sugar and sprinkled it over the buttered bread. Grandmother took the two pieces, placed them together and pressed down so the sugar would not fall off on the floor or table. I can't remember the last time I ate a sugar sandwich. But it sounds wonderful right now.

This was hospitality—a meaningful gesture to someone else. My grandmother did not have much, and it certainly was not fancy. But 78 years later, I remember how I felt in that very moment. The best, simplest treat ever.

Are you rolling your eyes and overdosing on sugar thoughts? Was she being bad by sending me on a sugar binge? My parents didn't always appreciate it much, either. But aren't we supposed to spoil grandchildren? Don't you? I do.

It surprised me to find a blogger[5] who ate sugar sandwiches when she was young. She includes recipes and variations of sugar sandwiches in many articles.

My grandmother's sweet spirit of giving and showing love and kind deeds didn't stop when we moved out of their home. They came in town to buy groceries at least once a week. They always stopped by on their way home and brought me and my brother and sister each a package of two Hostess Twinkies. We cut each Twinkie in half, sticking our tongues into the creamy white filling before eating. The three of us wrapped the uneaten half back up and placed it on the cabinet shelf. We were saving a few bites to have the next couple of days and continue savoring their sweetness as long as we could.

My grandparents and most farming families' major meal was at noon. They called it dinner. After everyone ate, my grandmother pulled her massive tablecloth back over the bowls of leftovers, which might have been corn on the cob, green beans, fried chicken and always applesauce. Yes, home-canned applesauce, using apples picked from the farm's orchard of apple trees. Everything was fresh: corn, beans, and a butchered chicken fried to perfection. I always wanted the chicken leg.

The evening meal they called supper. Grandmother pulled the tablecloth off and, voila, supper was served. The only thing she had to do was pour hot coffee and set out plates and silverware. At least that's how it looked to me. I shall never forget my grandmother's table.

Friends and family sat and talked for hours around that table during the supper hour. They discussed farm work, politics, and church.

I'll confess, I didn't care much for eating leftovers. Sometimes, I nibbled at the food and pushed it around on my plate, not wanting what they offered.

My grandmother, suspected I was hungry,

"You want some peanut butter and syrup?"

"Yes, I want peanut butter and syrup."

Early in the spring, my grandfather tapped sap from their maple trees in the nearby woods. Grandmother would slow boil the sap to make the yummiest syrup. They would pour the syrup in little jugs and store to use the rest of the year.

As she opened the jug of syrup and a jar of peanut butter, my mouth was watering with anticipation. She took a spoon full of creamy peanut butter and dropped it in a small bowl along with the maple syrup and whisked them together. This made the ingredients creamy and spreadable.

A simple and nutritious supper made with a slice of homemade bread, slathered with a peanut butter/syrup mixture. She cut it up in child-sized pieces so I could eat them with a fork. Oh my, what a meal for a four-year-old granddaughter. I will never forget those nights and that loving deed.

Our sons and I ate peanut butter and maple syrup many times for dinner when Bob was out of town. I put lots of peanut butter on two slices of bread, because I thought we needed the protein. I can't ever remember Bob eating this treat with us. He would shake his head and walk away.

Today, you may consider that to be very unhealthy. But if you use organic or pure maple syrup along with peanut butter that only has peanuts and a pinch of salt, it will be a good snack.

My Mentor

Our move to the small town of Orange, Indiana, before I started first grade was unsettling. The 3-block walk to school scared me. I had to wear glasses, and it humiliated me when kids called me "four eyes." My class met in a gigantic building with tons of people, or so I thought, and at least a gazillion stair steps connected the three floors. That terrified me.

Majestic maple trees surrounded our home, and lush green grass covered the vast yard. An enormous garden laden with vegetables, fruit trees, and beds of colorful flowers drew visitors many evenings. Although my dad was a rural letter carrier, his hobby was raising roses and over 300 bushes burst into glorious bloom each summer.

The church where we worshipped stood tall across the street from our house. I didn't enjoy climbing a dozen steps to get in the front door, but I was happy once inside the sanctuary. That is where I learned to worship and sing hymns.

Just north on the other corner of our little block, lived our neighbor, Mrs. Cross. She had a garden prolific with blooming perennial flowers. Her house had–two white swings, several white rocking chairs, and potted flowers and ferns along the porch edge. A perfect spot, on balmy summer evenings for neighbors to stop and visit, the porch seemed to beckon, "Come, sit a spell".

When people asked who had the greatest influence on my life, I remember a calm, saintly lady named Mrs. Cross.

Growing up, I'm not sure I remember hearing the word mentor spoken or seeing the term written in a book. But today, I know Mrs. Cross was my mentor.

Every Sunday morning, Mrs. Cross, a widow, walked the block and a half to church, carrying a big Bible. She climbed steps to the sanctuary, greeting people along the way, and sat in the same pew week after week.

In the evenings during the summer months, after laboring all day in her garden and backyard, Mrs. Cross laid a special cushion on her front porch swing seat. She always sat at the end of the one swing. A perfect spot to relax and wave to friends as they walked or drove by in the evening.

As a schoolgirl, I climbed up on the swing and dangled my legs off the seat's edge. But as I grew older, I could sit and push the swing by myself. A proud accomplishment. Every time I stopped with my parents to visit Mrs. Cross, I loved listening to her stories of growing up, ministry, and life.

Whenever we stopped by in the wintertime, Mrs. Cross welcomed us into her parlor. Around the glowing and crackling fire were groups of chairs, tables, lamps, and bookshelves overflowing with books. Lots of books. An antique clock on the mantle would tick-tock every second. It mesmerized me as a young child.

Her Bible lay open on the table with a giant magnifying glass laid across the pages. This quiet spot for study and prayer was a special place for Mrs. Cross.

Sometimes I rode my bike past her house and jumped off, running up the steps and sitting on Mrs. Cross's swing; yearning to listen and hear her Godly wisdom. God knew my future and was setting the stage.

Mrs. Cross was planting the seeds of what my ministry life might hold for many decades.

I remember, as a young girl, getting nervous when Mrs. Cross answered or spoke. Still, she was always kind, and I respected her teaching me simple tasks,

cutting a flower, straightening a cupboard, sweeping a walk. and heating a pan of water for tea. She helped me cultivate life skills, often using Scripture references as she talked. My mother taught me many things, but the words coming from Mrs. Cross made the instructions more palatable and meaningful.

I loved hearing stories about the ministry she and her husband shared. Mrs. Cross loved people and loved God. She made time for me. I trusted her. I treasured those times swinging on her porch swing. It was the perfect place to share dreams. This saintly woman encouraged me to do my best and work hard. She encouraged me to pray and listen to God's voice calling.

I hoped to major in classical piano performance and become a concert pianist; I never intended to marry a preacher. Her questions challenged me to consider several options and inspired me as we sat on the porch.

Mrs. Cross was planting the seeds of what my ministry life might hold for many decades.

After I left for college, Mrs. Cross sent encouraging notes on a postcard. I saved those notes for years.

My freshman year of college, I purchased a box of Christmas cards printed on black paper. The card featured gold wise men on the front. It was the prettiest Christmas card I ever saw, and I mailed one to Mrs. Cross because of her example of Christian love. During my Christmas break, I stopped to visit Mrs. Cross and spotted the card I sent her. I remember her telling me that every year she displayed the cards as reminders to pray for the sender and sometimes send a note.

Not long after that visit, Mrs. Cross died. When I get to heaven, I will find her and tell her I married a preacher. We can share stories of life as preachers' wives. How will she respond? Will she wink and reply, "I've always known"? With a thankful heart, I will give her a warm hug for being a mentor that welcomed this schoolgirl to come sit awhile on her porch.

Did you have a Mrs. Cross in your life? Are you a Mrs. Cross in a young lady's life?

What is a Mentor?

As an experienced and trusted advisor, you might encourage someone. I never envisioned myself as a mentor. But I learned how from my mentor, Mrs. Cross.

1. Have lunch or coffee with a young lady to encourage, listen, and pray for her. Your life's experiences may mean so much to the person sitting with you.
2. Listen and encourage a lady that just moved to your city. To help her get settled, offer to drive her to the best shopping areas and fun places.
3. Have lunch with a young professional, high school, or college student. Pray out loud for her needs. Time invested with younger girls is rewarding. What a blessing to watch them mature, earn degrees, marry, and have babies.
4. Send a text message of encouragement to a young lady. Surprise her with a note of encouragement. It doesn't have to be every week or month. Comment on her Facebook and Instagram pages. Remember her birthday.

The Porch

I miss the front porch and the lawn chairs in our backyards and when people used to stop and chat after dinner. Today, we live hurried lives, seldom calling a neighbor or friend. Don't you wish we could find a moment to stop and sip a glass of iced tea and sit on the porch swing? What happened to those peaceful, slower times of talking with family and friends?

Claude Stephens, an avid front porch advocate, established the Porch Sitter's Union[6] in Louisville, Kentucky in 1999. The Union says people do not need a front porch. A terrace, balcony, small portico will work—even an open garage door.

Kristin Schell, author of *The Turquoise Table*[7], placed a picnic table in her front yard. She went outside every morning to sit and pray. People stopped by. She met people that lived in her neighborhood. Through doing this outreach, she learned the differences between entertaining and hospitality. Kristin realized hospitality is not what we're doing. It's who we are.

I admire those who take time to stop and talk with people. How about when picking up your mail or taking out the trash? What a perfect time to say hello. That's showing hospitality without even going in the house.

Sharing with Others

I couldn't keep my dad anymore. It was too difficult for me to manage him, myself, and ministry. When I said "Daddy, I can't keep you long term." He replied with three words. "Yes, I know." How freeing it was to hear those loving words from my dad. I had suffered a stroke the year earlier and to have him live with us could be difficult.

He was living alone and needed to make changes. He decided on his own to sell his house and move to a retirement home. I knew this was a good move. He was a people-person and loved to tell stories and jokes. He wasn't bashful about his faith—never hesitating to ask someone where they stood with the Lord.

When it came time for him to move, I met my brother and sister at our dad's house. We spent several days sorting through things. It was bittersweet. All three of us thought of Dad's rose garden and hoped to take a few rose bushes to our homes. Those bushes lived and thrived for 30 to 40 years with the care my dad gave them.

Over the years, I watched how he would snip off stems with blooms and picked off thorns before handing a rose to ladies who stopped to see the gardens. He took small bouquets to folks in the hospital or a bouquet to church. There was always a vase of roses on our kitchen table.

It was an exciting day when my sister dropped off 12 prized rose bushes at my home. To keep the tradition of sharing with others, I hired a gardener to create a small rose garden in our yard. I enjoyed sharing those lovely flowers with people.

CHAPTER 4

It's More Than a Table

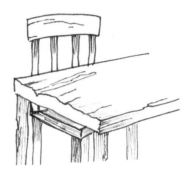

"Share with the Lord's people in need. Practice hospitality."

Romans 12:13, NIV

CAN YOU IMAGINE if our kitchen and dining room tables could talk, the stories they would share? Stories of spills and burnt meals, of missed ingredients and yummy desserts. The most memorable stories would be of family, friends, and guests who shared precious conversations over the years.

Our First Dining Room Table and Chairs

As a young bride, new dining room furniture did not appear on the list of needs for our humble home. One can dream, right? I dreamed some time we would have a solid wood dining room table, and people would gather and share their lives.

After the first year in our new home, my parents gave us a round folding table. No chairs, just the table. It thrilled me to place the table under the light in our dining room. Now, we could walk through without banging our head on the low-hanging crystal chandelier. I draped it with a large, round tablecloth that hung to the floor, and a floral centerpiece and candles that glowed when lit. It was perfect, even without chairs.

A year later, an older lady gave us her old mahogany table and six chairs. I was ecstatic. They were in great condition. The chair's legs, though scratched from use, were sturdy. I wiped them with Old English furniture polish to cover the nicks and scratches, and they looked new.

I pulled a chair out from the table to sit a moment. Who graced this table in earlier years? Were their conversations filled with laughter? Prayers? Were there intense table fellowship discussions? Did folks lean in and put their elbows on the table, so they didn't miss a single word?

I couldn't help but wonder who would sit at that table. We wanted family and friends to share a meal, tell stories, laugh and cry together, dream and pray, even confess wrongdoings. We needed those times of table fellowship.

Twenty years passed, and we moved, taking that table full of scratches and scars to a new place. I had it refinished and wiped clean. When a furniture refinisher dipped and refinished the table, it was near perfect. And it reminded me of when we ask forgiveness of our sins and Jesus washes us clean through baptism, we are made new.

For forty years I cared for that table, eventually relegating the worn chairs to the basement.

Our son and his wife offered their dining room chairs to us. Theirs were in storage while building a new home. We said yes, and the chairs brightened up our room. I no longer worried a chair might collapse when a guest sat to eat.

Months later we were traveling to Philadelphia where Bob was to be speaking at a conference. I said to my friend Barbara, "My favorite furniture store is in the King of Prussia Mall, let's stop there." What a pleasant surprise to discover our hotel was only minutes away.

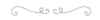

Remember, it's not the food eaten at the table, but the company seated there.

I walked into the store and spotted Scottish red plaid fabric draped in an enormous doorway. It shocked me! There was the material I dreamed about for dining room chairs. I searched for a year or more through magazines and stores, knowing when I saw red Scottish plaid material it was right. I walked on through the store and to my surprise—there was my dream table. A solid, walnut-wood table, surrounded by six red Scottish plaid parson chairs and two host chairs in the same red plaid. Was I dreaming? Or was this real?

I glanced at the price tag on one chair and thought, "Oh, no. It's too much money!" My friend came into the store searching for me and gave a hearty approval of the furniture.

The store decorator had preset the table with white chargers and blue-willow plates at each place setting. The look was exquisite. This was what I had envisioned. The red plaid gave it a hint of masculinity, but classy and striking for ladies.

I talked with the sales assistant and the pieces were on sale with a big percentage price cut. I needed to get my husband in there and quick. I couldn't stop thinking about that dining room table and chairs.

Bob liked everything too, and he knew we needed to do something. We discussed a plan. We talked further after we got home and decided. Yes, it was ours. Two months later, our dining room furniture arrived.

It was over twelve years ago that I ordered that table and chairs. You may say that it is foolish to spend money on an elaborate dining room table. You don't understand. A table is a place people share their lives, their dreams, and their disappointments. A place where strangers become friends, as walls come down and they receive acceptance and hope.

Over a thousand preachers have plopped down on those red plaid chairs and put their elbows on our table. There have been countless family gatherings around our table celebrating birthdays and holiday dinners and "just because" days. Coaches, professors, college presidents, political figures, governors, friends, and neighbors have shared meals with us at our table.

My focus is not the table or the delicious food eaten. Instead, my focus is on those putting their elbows on the table. It's the lively conversations and robust laughter, the inspiring stories and sweet prayers. God has blessed us as we have shared with hundreds of people. They love the time of fellowship, laughter, prayers, the stories told and the encouragement received.

Remember, it's not the food eaten at the table, but the company seated there.

The Table's Next Home

Our dear, old table needed a new home. I posted a message on my Facebook page, "Solid Mahogany Antique Table, free to a good home."

Within seconds of posting on Facebook, a young, single lady from our church sent a reply. Becky wanted our table. Even though I loved and enjoyed the times around that table, I imagined Becky's friends gathering around and putting elbows on her table. They would laugh and talk, sing and pray, and lean in for times of sweet fellowship.

"When Jesus wanted to explain to his followers what his forthcoming death was all about, he did not give them a theory, a model, a metaphor, or any other such thing; he gave them a meal."

—N.T. Wright, **The Day the Revolution Began**[8]

"One of the most important spiritual disciplines for us to recover in the kind of world in which we live is the discipline of table fellowship."[9]

—Barry D. Jones

CHAPTER 5

Snow on the Mountain

"They broke bread in their homes and ate
together with glad and sincere hearts."

Acts 2:46, NIV

OUR FAMILY'S FAVORITE meal is a Polynesian dish called Snow on the Mountain.[10] A colonel in the Army gave a copy of the recipe to my friend, and she gave me a copy.

Dinner guests build a mountain, starting with a rice base, adding the creamed chicken and mushroom sauce. There are nine different toppings to spoon over the mountain of rice.

Laugh at Disaster

I still cringe remembering a horrible goof-up, not once but twice, as I prepared our family's favorite recipe for company.

Our trip to the Holy Land with three other couples was unforgettable. We wanted to say thank you for inviting us, so we invited them to our house for dinner, served Snow on the Mountain, and gave each couple a photo album commemorating our trip. (A surprise gift is always fun for both the giver and receiver.)

It was the day of our dinner. Early that morning, I began preparing the food. Everything needed to be stored in the refrigerator until time to eat. But first, leftovers stored in the refrigerator needed thrown away.

I began forcing a dish full of rice into the disposal. There was dead silence when I flipped on the disposal switch. Nothing happened—no whining, no grinding, nothing. Oh my, the drain was full of leftover rice! What could I do with a clogged drain and six people coming to dinner? How was I supposed to know you never put leftover rice in the disposal? Never doing that again.

Since there was no plumber available, I resorted to the powder room sink for hot and cold water and a drain. Bob was my super helper, runner, chopper, and cleaner-upper. He worked at the powder room sink, washing vegetables and dishes the entire morning.

Have you ever thought about how often you turn the water on at your kitchen sink? During meal preparation, you are washing dishes and cleaning up pots and pans. How many times do you need to use the disposal or wash your hands? I was so glad we started preparation early.

The time for the couples to arrive approached at breakneck speed. I was trying to clean up while stirring the creamed chicken sauce. By then, eight of us were standing at the kitchen island. I love people doing that, but sometimes conversations can be a major distraction. As we were relaying the day's events, the dreadful odor of burning cream sauce filled the kitchen.

I shoved a stopper into the clogged sink drain and turned on the faucet, placing the pan in water a few moments to slow the cooking. Scorched food is one problem a cook doesn't need when three couples are watching.

We salvaged just enough cream sauce for our meal.

Guests began building their mountain with the food set up buffet style and gathered around the table. Everyone enjoyed eating Snow on the Mountain, as we laughed and talked about the trip.

While cleaning up, I thought about the scorched cream sauce. I could have cried, or yelled—or worse, cussed. Disasters happen, so we buck up, swallow hard, and keep on smiling.

"If we are transparent, admit our mistakes, and laugh about it, it helps to break down barriers."
—Bob Russell

It's humbling when we invite people into our homes and they see us, flaws and all. It's the risk of hospitality. But there's something special about sharing disastrous moments. Everyone breathes when it's not perfect. Maybe it gives them permission to be imperfect, too.

Mistakes remind us of the brokenness of life. No one is perfect. Neither is any meal, guest, or host. It shows the brokenness of life and points us to Jesus.

And the Mountain is . . .

Yes, I have my share of mishaps with food preparation—often occurring when guests are on their way. I've prepared Snow on the Mountain for our immediate family dozens of times. I don't recall a mishap for any of those special gatherings.

We were driving home from one of Bob's speaking engagements and stopped to get a quick bite to eat. We met a delightful young couple who were members at our church. They too were returning from a trip, and we invited them to join us.

On our way home, we talked about the couple we just met. We wanted to introduce them to two young married couples we knew and cook dinner. I emailed everyone to see if we could pull off this venture and everyone was available. So, I made an Evite and sent it to each couple. I was ecstatic when we received confirmation that everyone could come.

A Sample of the Evite

"They broke bread in their homes and ate
together with glad and sincere hearts."
Acts 2:46 NIV

Dinner at the Russell's
August 23, 2021
6:30 pm
1234 Seventh Street
Anytown, State
123-456-7890
Casual Attire
Looking forward to seeing you.
List names of guests invited.
RSVP to name@www.com or 123-456-7890

The appointed night came, and we were ready to experience a fun evening. Food sliced, chopped, and placed in bowls. Chicken cooked and stirred into the cream sauce. I placed everything on the kitchen island in the order of serving. A printed, framed menu was on the counter listing the ingredients. I set ceramic holders in front of each of the nine bowls, naming the topping ingredient.

We began gathering our guest's plates after eating the salad.

Before we begin to assemble the "mountains," I always tell the recipe's origin. As I spoke those words, I glanced over to the island counter and in horror realized I forgot the rice!

My mind was racing as I thought, Dear Lord, let there be rice in the pantry. Ahh, Minute Rice to the rescue, as I yanked it from the shelf. "Go on asking questions, give me six minutes, I will listen while fixing the rice."

Waiting for the water to boil was an eternity. I poured the grains of rice into the hot water, covered the pan with a lid, and waited five minutes. Another eternity. Yay, the rice was ready.

"Pretending you're perfect, people will admire you from a distance for a little while. But if you openly admit your imperfections, they will identify with you and love you up close forever."

Bob Russell

What is it with my Snow on the Mountain dinners? Was I trying to impress someone?

Obviously, I wasn't thinking clearly as I placed ceramic signs on the counter noting the different foods and toppings. That should have triggered my memory that I had forgotten the rice, even before our guests arrived.

Why did I forget the rice? I've prepared that dish dozens of times and never messed up the recipe. You know, sometimes we just forget!

It's hard enough today for young couples to open their homes to dinner guests. These three couples open their homes to groups from church and their neighborhoods often. I was thankful it didn't destroy their wish to host others. I hope it left an impression that things will be okay, even though imperfect.

That evening, I learned a lesson about preparation. Write a list of things needed and things to do several days in advance. Set out serving dishes, label their use, and check in the pantry for supplies. And I will always have a box of rice in my pantry.

Not to scare you, but it's inevitable that mistakes will happen. Remember—even great cooks make mistakes, and not everything will be perfect. You may forget the seasoning, an ingredient, or the whole dish, as I did. Admit it, smile, and try to make the best of things.

Snow on the Mountain with Chuck Colson

Each year in February, Christian Church megachurch pastors and their wives gather at a conference for inspiration, laughter, and fun. One year, our friend Chuck Colson was the guest speaker.

We became acquainted with Chuck Colson through a mutual friend. Visiting with him and having him in our home several times was a blessing. He was a great encourager to Bob and his ministry.

One evening, when Chuck was in our home, I served Snow on the Mountain for dinner. He loved it and even went back for seconds. Before he left the house, he asked me for the recipe. I was honored.

Before Chuck began his inspiring message at the conference, he greeted the audience and shared about the dinner of Snow on the Mountain he ate with us. I was embarrassed, yet pleased. Guests appreciate when you do something special. After they leave, and you close the front door, remember, it's about the person who sat in the chair and—just maybe—about the food.

It's not the food or the table setting that creates a memorable meal, but the way we show our guests respect and kindness.

CHAPTER 6

A Tea Party in a Maasai Hut

"A leader must be well-thought-of, committed to his
wife, cool and collected, accessible, and hospitable.

I Timothy 3:2 MSG

WILDERNESS COUNTRY? WILD beasts? Maasai Land?

Missionaries wanted Bob to speak at a retreat in Mombasa,
Kenya, and veteran mission-traveling friends, Russ and Jane
Summay, agreed to go with us. Two of the Kenyan missionary
couples our church supported lived and worked in Maasai
land. We wanted to visit them also. Nervous and excited, we
said yes.

Africa, here we come!

Landing in Nairobi, Kenya, we longed for rest from the

lengthy flight. It wasn't easy adjusting to a different time zone. Eager for a special evening supper, we chose the Carnivore Restaurant on the outskirts of Nairobi. Their chefs grill wild game on Maasai swords. They offered us gazelle, warthog, crocodile, wildebeest, and zebra as food choices. Guests stuffed with yummy food were the restaurant's goal and when finished, people waved a white flag, proclaiming, "Full!" What a memorable evening.

Deep inside I wondered, 'do I want to be a guest in a Maasai hut?'

The next morning, we were to start our drive to Narok, spend the night, and then continue on to Maasai Land. Treacherous roads and traveling up a riverbed in a four-wheel vehicle became a bone-rattling ride that left us exhausted. We drove through areas of flattened bushes and trees trampled by stampeding elephant herds. It resembled a war zone. Wild zebra and other wild beasts wandered across the countryside. I hoped they'd keep their distance.

Hours later, we arrived at the missionary's home in bush country. Grateful for this modest and efficient place, we unpacked our luggage and prepared for the week's stay.

Jane and I both packed several skirts. Maasai women do not wear jeans or pants. They consider it immodest. We decided it was best to wear skirts and planned on leaving them with the missionaries to distribute after we returned home.

We offered to help with dinner preparations. The first thing we cleaned was a fresh head of cabbage in bleach water because Maasai tribes use human waste to fertilize their vegetable gardens. Our hostess, who was an experienced cook, took great precaution in preparing our food.

The Villagers held their worship services on a grassy area at the edge of the village. People sat on large logs while others sat on the ground. The message Bob delivered from God's Word through an interpreter made listening difficult for those of us who didn't speak or understand Swahili.

An elder of the tribe invited us to have tea and meet his family. A tea party in a hut? This unexpected visit was a big strain for me, as it wasn't on my to-do list to have tea in a Maasai's hut. We agreed to go.

Earlier, our missionary host told us horror stories of enormous cockroaches crawling on the ceilings of the huts. When spending the night in a hut, the men shove their pant legs deep into boots they are wearing so bugs can't creep up their legs while they sleep. I shudder just recalling those words. If you shine your flashlight on the ceiling, the bugs crawl everywhere. Wait a moment, they wear their boots to bed? I hate roaches!

My mother said I was the only child she knew that played in a sandbox and stayed clean. Is it possible to stay clean in a hut with a dirt floor?

Deep inside I wondered, 'do I want to be a guest in a Maasai hut?'

Our drive to the village was over a narrow, roughly hewn lane full of holes, reminding me of a rugged cow path. I was eager to get out and stretch my legs. Bob opened the door of the four-wheeler; I grabbed my skirt and drew it up, slid from the Jeep's front seat, stepping into mud and dung. No green lawns here. Animal and people-trampled mud was everywhere we looked.

Villagers' cows searched for food while their calves kept close by and chickens pecked for tasty morsels. A group of squealing children ran everywhere, and stench from smoke and cattle permeated the air. Our throats ached.

In a clearing, just beyond a grove of trees, were the village's loaf-shaped huts. How intriguing to discover that the women built them, not the men.

They used mud along with grass, sticks, manure, and urine to create the hut's walls. Roofs needed a durable substance to be water repellent, and the grass and dung mixture worked. They didn't have windows. The only outside light shone through the doorway.

The elder led us to his family's hut. Unaware of the damp earth that squished between little brown toes, his children rushed up with greetings. The custom is to bow their heads and wait. We patted the top of each one's curly hair and repeated, "Supa, Supa", which means hello. Their fly-covered eyelashes and toothy grins caught our attention.

As we entered through the narrow opening to the elder's home, it shocked us to see half of the hut was a barn stall! Here, a cow and her calf will stay out of harm's way. The family living quarters included a fire pit for cooking and a hole in the ceiling for smoke to escape.

They formed their beds, using long twigs wrapped together with grass fibers. Unusual though basic furniture pieces added to the living quarters. Narrow wooden benches provided seating along the wall. Sitting on the stick bed, Jane and I tucked our skirts under our legs to protect them from dragging on the earthen floor.

The elder's wife reached into a tiny storage cabinet for several chipped, dented tin mugs. She banged them on her hip as if to shake something out. I watched, wondering, 'Will we be drinking out of those cups?' She yanked a corner of her skirt up, using it to wipe out each mug. The scarred and dirty mugs were now clean and will soon be full of warm tea.

Would I pour hot tea into a chipped cup?

A small pot perched on a grate over the smoldering fire. Our hostess picked the pot up and poured Chai into each cup. They made it with fresh cow's milk, sugar, and strong tea. I swallowed hard, wondering if boiling hot tea could sterilize the mugs as I raised one to my lips for a sip.

There was an awkward stillness surrounding us as we sipped tea.

I wondered as we drank if other people could hear the little calf peeing nearby. Jane and I giggled under our breath as it reminded us Maasai cattle are villagers' prized possessions.

Through our interpreter, the elder spoke to Jane, "Is your house like this"?

A deathly silence filled the space until Jane said, "Well, our roof is a little higher."

I choked back tears. Do we have the slightest clue how blessed we are? It shook me to see this family and how they were so thankful for their meager but grace-filled home. With kindness, the Maasai couple had shared their tea. Their respectful greeting and unselfish gestures of hospitality honored us.

Did they drink tea? I don't even remember. Not enough mugs? Is it their culture to stare and grin while only guests drink the Chai?

I've wondered since then, am I gracious to strangers? Do I express kindness to individuals who do not speak my language? Am I kind? Am I a humble servant? Do I share my resources?

Would I pour hot tea into a chipped cup?

I prefer things organized and ready. A bouquet on the dinner table, candles glowing, and nice table settings. That's my preference. Yet, am I forgetting something more relevant?

I appreciate how people open their homes, even though circumstances are not perfect.

For others, having people for tea will put them in a tizzy. Since my life has been full of unexpected happenings, centered on food, I've learned that "Simple is as simple does." People enjoy being treated as family, being served simple meals on simple plates at a simple table. Nothing fancy. Just simple.

So, which one will it be? Tea in a fancy china cup or a chipped enamel coffee mug or a Styrofoam cup? Chances are that people are equally as happy with a Styrofoam cup. Quick and simple. The tea will still taste the same.

Remember, people matter. How we greet, treat, and speak with people is hospitality.

And what is the most important thing? "It's who's in the chair!"

Simple Hospitality Ideas

1. Invite a friend for a cup of tea.
2. Offer assorted ice cream flavors and add toppings.
3. Brew coffee and slice a piece of coffeecake or pumpkin bread.
4. Share a yummy cup of soup, salad, and bread.
5. Have a salad supper with a choice of greens, veggies, fruit, nuts, meats, and dressings.
6. Charcuterie board with assorted fruit, cheese, and crackers. Some grocery stores are making prepared trays.

CHAPTER 7

Risky, Radical, and Generous Hospitality

"May the LORD now show you kindness and faithfulness, and I too will show you the same favor because you have done this."

2 Samuel 2:6, NIV

IN FIFTEEN MINUTES, my sweet, compassionate husband was bringing someone home he found sleeping under the overhang of our church building. Thoughts swirled through my head as I hung up the phone. What is he doing? I'm not ready for this!

Hospitality is when you make others welcome in your space, your home. To me, bringing a homeless man into our home was radical hospitality.

A Homeless Guest

My chest tightened as I raced upstairs to grab sheets and blankets, towels, and clean clothes for the man.

Bob's home office doubled as a guest room. We furnished it with a chair, desk, lamp, and a sofa bed. I hurriedly pulled off the cushions, yanked open the bed, and put on clean sheets. Rushing to beat the clock, I checked the bathroom for soap, deodorant, a toothbrush, and other essentials.

Bob stepped into the house with our unknown guest following, his eyes nervously darting back and forth. He was dirty, unshaven, and in desperate need of a haircut. He grunted a word under his breath when we greeted him.

We showed the man his room and urged him to shower. I sprayed disinfectant to get rid of the rank odor while he showered. By now I was a nervous wreck as I thought, 'What have we done? Are we safe?'

It annoyed me having to gather up the wet towels and dirty, stinky clothing, as I gagged from the rancid odor. It was far worse than sweaty, smelly football uniforms. His were intolerable. I put them through the washer's hot water cycle three times to get them clean.

I filled a plate for him with warmed leftovers from our evening dinner. In the meantime, our children wanted their nightly chocolate chip cookies and a glass of milk. As our guest gulped his meal, I prepared a snack for everyone.

It embarrassed me as I watched how our boys stared at the man seated across the table from them. We asked him to join in our evening Bible story and prayer. The four of us prayed out loud for him and he listened, saying nothing.

It was getting late and time to go to bed. Our bedrooms were upstairs, and the guest bedroom was downstairs. It scared me to host this stranger in our home. I was uncomfortable, thinking

Bob better take this guest somewhere else in the morning. What was he thinking? The devil was doing a number on me.

My mind continued to spin. Was I pretending to be hospitable? I didn't close my eyes the entire night. Jesus would have welcomed him. How long would he stay? Questions, questions, questions swirled through my mind. I tried to go to sleep.

God loves us 24/7, and he welcomes us whether we are clean or dirty, stinky or perfumed. Did I welcome this filthy, smelly man as Jesus would? I didn't. Did the anxiousness of the past several hours block out a blessing for me and my family and our guest? I think so.

The next morning, our guest was more talkative as he plopped on the sofa, making himself at home. He flipped through the TV channels and messed with the boys' toys appearing too comfortable. I finally breathed when Bob said it was time to go.

We learned our guest used to attend our youth program before he dropped out of high school and ran away from home.

We heard someone lived in the scoreboard at the high school football field behind our church. That night, we realized the boarder in the school scoreboard was our house guest. I ached for his family.

Bob talked with him about going home and finding a job. He gave the young man cash, called his parents, then drove him to their house.

I've wondered how God used that night of radical hospitality long ago to begin our guest's healing? Did the Bible reading and prayer time give him the courage he needed? Encouragement to move home, find work, and go to church?

Did the few hours with our family mean something? I pray that evening was a turning point for our guest. It was for me. It opened my eyes and heart to take the risk, trust in God, have faith, and be careful.

Take the Risk

It may come easy for people to reach out to others with radical hospitality. A family member might bring someone home they met on the street corner or in a shelter. That is radical. Sometimes folks never lock their door. To me, that is risky and radical.

People strolling after a neighborhood Bible study may see a group of guys standing on the street corner and strike up a conversation. That is risky. Particularly if the group of guys are making drug deals in the shadows of a streetlight.

When an opportunity comes along, go for it. Trust in God and have faith.

Risky hospitality can be unsafe in places today. Mission work is radical and risky. To open your home to a group of strangers is radical. Yes, God is with you, and I commend you, but it makes me nervous.

We show radical hospitality at church by greeting a person or family we've never met and inviting them to eat at our home after the service.

Plan a neighborhood potluck dinner and invite the new family across the street. Ask them to go to church as your guest on Sunday.

What about your hairstylist or nail tech or doctor? Invite them to church and lunch afterward.

Plan an outing with your Bible study group and take treats to first responders. Pray with the firefighters and police officers and invite them to your church service.

Ask the server at your table in a restaurant if it's okay to pray for them right then and leave a big tip. 30%?

Have you ever considered setting up a grill and cooking hotdogs and hamburgers at a park in an urban district and offering free sandwiches to anyone who stops? A group of career guys from our church do this in different neighborhoods. They feed people and invite them to church.

You may say that these suggestions are not necessarily risky hospitality. Those people don't stand on the street corner or sleep under a bridge. True.

Whether on a street corner, in a park, at church, or at a restaurant, the opportunities to speak to individuals about Jesus are endless.

It is hard for me to be outgoing and talk to a stranger. My preference is to be quiet and listen to those interacting. I have read books and listened to speakers that encouraged me to reach out to others.

Is your temperament more of an introvert? Uncomfortable talking about Jesus and inviting folks to attend church with you? I understand. There are times it's easy and sometimes not.

When an opportunity comes along, go for it. Trust in God and have faith.

Unexpected Generosity

When you are picking up your order at a fast-food drive-thru, ask how much the check is for the person's order in the car behind you. Pay for it and drive away. That's generous hospitality extended to an unsuspecting stranger. Don't you wonder what their comments will be?

On one day, I was the recipient of unexpected generosity. I drove to the cleaners to drop off Bob's shirts and stopped by Starbucks to get a treat for my grandson. The drive-thru line was lengthy, thinking, 'ah, a perfect chance to catch up on a couple texts'.

They took my order, and I waited. Longer than usual. When I drove up to the window, the barista greeted me, "No charge, ma'am. You are the fourth car, and a person ahead of you paid for the four cars behind her."

Oh, my goodness, it's my lucky day. How sweet of them. I wanted to say thanks but my benefactor was long gone. Wasn't that a kind gesture? Thank you, Lord, for whoever the generous person might be, and bless them today.

Do that sometime. It's exciting to be generous to an unsuspecting person.

The $20 Challenge

Friends shared this unusual gesture of being radical with generosity. As they shared their story, we could sense the excitement and blessings they received by being generous to an unsuspecting person.

They heard Pastor Chip Ingram speak and got his book, *The Genius of Generosity*[11]. He challenged people to give a twenty-dollar bill to an unsuspecting person. Imagine how a person would react? Our friends tried this when guests visited them, handing each person a new twenty-dollar bill and the book by Chip Ingram. Plus, issuing the challenge!

The four guests each, and their hosts, took one week to give their twenty-dollar bill away. Then they gathered again to share their stores of generosity.

I want to try this at one of our dinner gatherings. I plan to stop by our bank to get several crisp twenty-dollar bills to give to each of our guests. Reaching out to others can be a rewarding few moments.

Here are some ideas of who to pass the $20 along to:

- A housekeeper who cleans your hotel rooms.
- The busser who clears tables in a restaurant.
- A person who works hard, but their pay is little.
- The college student scanning and bagging your groceries.
- What about the lady waiting in the grocery store's checkout lane? She may need an encouraging word and extra cash?
- Remember the mailman. Christmas is a perfect time to give an inspirational book and a twenty-dollar bill tucked inside the pages.

Generosity Throughout the Year

Thanksgiving morning is a perfect time to take your family to a soup kitchen in your city. What a nice holiday memory when all of you serve together and give encouragement to those eating a meal.

For years, our family's Christmas Eve tradition was taking gifts to a needy family. A teacher gave me the names, clothing sizes, and specific needs of a particular family. We bought each child clothes along with puzzles, games, and books. We included a Christian book for them to read for their family devotions and a snack of cookies or brownies.

One year the teacher told me she kept a hairbrush in her desk drawer. She used that hairbrush to brush a young girl's hair when she got to school. The teacher suggested we buy the girl her own for one of her gifts. Giving a hairbrush as a Christmas gift was odd to me. But I got one!

Another year she suggested new toothbrushes and toothpaste for our needy family.

Each year, when we started driving to a family's home, our boys were excited. But riding back to our house was different. Now they were quiet. Our trip of generosity left an impression on them. They would ask questions and comment about what they saw or how people acted. A perfect chance for us to talk about being generous to others.

Why not try opening your home to college interns and traveling college groups? Those inexperienced young people may be nervous and lonely and unsure of themselves. Encouragement and a home-cooked meal blesses students. Your younger children will love having them too.

You may think that generosity and hospitality don't go together, but showing hospitality with generosity to others will bless you and your family. Studies show that giving to and helping others benefits us.

CHAPTER 8

Around the Table

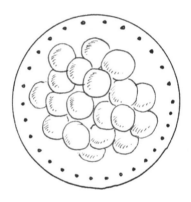

"When one of the Pharisees invited Jesus to have dinner with him, he went to the Pharisee's house and reclined at the table."

Luke 7:36, NIV

THERE ARE PLENTY of resources to make food preparation easier. Thank goodness for caterers, carryout, and the deli at a small local market. And now, those family meal home delivery services that are available! Wow!

Colorful Solo plastic plates and cups are my new best friends. They are quick to grab from a pantry shelf and make cleanup easy. I've learned to keep a stack of supplies handy for unexpected moments.

Keep It Simple

I often serve brownies or chocolate chip cookies warm from the oven to make up for my lack of cooking. There is nothing better, when gathered around the table with family and friends, than laughing, talking, and eating warm chocolate chip cookies with a glass of milk.

At one of those spur-of-the-moment family gatherings, I overheard my 8-year-old grandson say, "My grandmother makes the best brownies and chocolate chip cookies in the world!"

It's not true. They're never perfect. Sometimes they're too crunchy because I baked them too long. Still, it meant lots to hear him say it.

Our grandchildren are older now, and they enjoy talking and taking part in discussions at the table. We've discussed politics, sports, history, church, Scripture, family, school news, etc. Those things we discuss and share at a family table, help make the family bond stronger. Sometimes we share stories and secrets that might never be told outside of those walls.

Becky Hand, a blogger and dietician, suggests eight reasons for eating together.[12]

1. Communication and well-being
2. Modeling manners
3. Expanding children's understanding of the world, one food at a time
4. Nourishment
5. Teaching self-sufficiency
6. Preventing destructive behaviors
7. Improving grades
8. Saving money

I laugh about numbers four and eight. How many of us will call the pizza shop for delivery? That's me! You think ordering a pizza with arugula will make it healthier? And number eight? Pizza being delivered may not save money, but it sure saves time.

What if following these guidelines was an actual test? Would I pass? It convicted me to work harder on each of those benefits. A peanut butter and jelly sandwich would be a quick meal with the boys. Especially if Bob was out of town. Oops!

The Importance of the Table

Pastor and author Leonard Sweet wrote in *From Tablet to Table,* "One thing that would dramatically change the world and help return us to our rootedness in Christ: bring back the table! What might happen if we made the table the most sacred object of furniture in every home. The table is the place where identity is born. It is the place where the story of our lives is told, remembered, and relived."

In the book, published in 2014, Sweet writes, "The average parent spends only 38.5 minutes per week in meaningful conversation with their children. We are losing the table."[13]

Tom Kersting, a counselor and author, wrote *Disconnected* six years later in 2020. He says, "During this digital age, the average time parents spend in meaningful conversation with their children is 3.5 minutes per week."[14] .

Isn't that unbelievable? 3.5 minutes per week? That's less than 30 seconds a day. And six years prior, it was 38.5 minutes per week.

Kersting continues,

> "Sitting down to dinner together is essential to developing deep, lasting family relationships. In today's drive-thru world, it is becoming less and less common, unfortunately. Make it your goal to eat together at least 3 nights a week.

"The dinner table and car rides are two of the most important places in the world for parents. They present the perfect opportunities to talk to our children about their day, see what's on their minds, and form connections with them."

Even as parents, we find ourselves glued to our tech devices, rather than finding time to sit at the table and have a meaningful conversation. Think about that for a moment. We can't find time to talk about our child's day at school? Or where you will pick them up from football practice? Even time to pray together? We have lost those meaningful moments. No wonder our children are dealing with anxiety, feelings of inadequacy, frustration, and suicide.

How about considering having everyone lay aside their devices and gather around the table to reconnect with family and learn hospitality?

To prepare for this book, I discovered several interesting statistics about eating together. 60 years ago, the average meal lasted 90 minutes. Today, that same meal takes less than 12 minutes. Talk about sad?

In Time magazine, Nancy Gibbs wrote an article about 'The Magic of the Family Meal'.[15]

Ms. Gibbs writes,

"There's something special about a shared meal, not some holiday blowout, not once in a while, but regularly, reliably that anchors a family even on nights when the food is fast and the talk cheap and everyone has some place they'd rather be."

The article continues: "Studies show the more often families eat together, the less likely kids are to smoke, drink, do drugs, get depressed, develop eating disorders and consider suicide, and the more likely they are to do well in school, delay having sex, eat their vegetables, learn big words and know which fork to use."

"Kids who eat most often with their parents are 40% more likely to say they get mainly A's and B's in school."

"So, pull up some chairs. Lose the TV. Let the phone go unanswered. And see where the moment takes you."

There are 76 references in the Bible to tables and over 1,200 to food.

At his birth, they laid Jesus in a feeding trough, a table for animals. At the last meal with his disciples, he broke bread at a table. The table is an important fixture in all of our lives.

Our Lord invites us to meet with Him at His table every Lord's Day. Your church may not have an actual communion table. When we partake at communion services, we can visualize taking the bread and juice together with Christians from all over the world.

Meals don't happen without planning. If a family gathering takes place, someone must be the 'doer', the planner. Since I'm the organizer in our family, I accept that I am the 'doer'. If someone doesn't step up and suggest getting together, it might never happen. I've discovered I'm often that someone.

We like for others to be the 'doer' sometimes. Somebody to plan a simple gathering with family or friends. Perhaps a family reunion gathering, and yes, that takes lots of work and organization. But could it be God's calling on our lives?

When I realized I was the 'doer', I was so thankful Bob

would come alongside me and suggest a gathering of folks and help. It has been fun being the 'doer'. Sure, it's hard work. There have been times I wish I hadn't said yes. The planning and budgeting are time-consuming. But the blessings from gathering around the table together are insurmountable.

Prayer at the Table

While rushing through a meal, discussing family issues or current events rarely occurred. When finished eating, before being excused from the table, I didn't have the boys pick up their dirty plates and put them in the dishwasher. We didn't always practice respectful manners either. Nor did I expect the boys to stay seated at the table after dinner when we had guests.

But we always prayed. Even if we were in a hurry. We thanked God for food and the day—asked for mercy and grace over an issue and for guests visiting with us. They were not long prayers as everyone wanted to eat. But we prayed.

I grew up saying, "God is great, God is good, let us thank him for our food, Amen". We were young and our prayers were often by rote. I remember my parents encouraging us to think deeper in gratitude and thanksgiving as we prayed.

When our boys were just learning to talk, we taught them that prayer. It is easy for little ones to repeat. But as our children grow older and learn Bible stories and scripture, it's important to us as parents that we pray and be an example for our children as we express thanks.

Today, I love hearing my grandchildren pray for their food, friends, parents, siblings and cousins, a test, their dad's safety, and the day. Sometimes they pray for everybody. Sometimes it's just a few words. But they are praying.

In many homes, prayer isn't said at mealtime. Did you ever think why we pray for our meal? One is acknowledging God's goodness and greatness. Expressing thanks for God's provision, our homes, and food. And realizing how much He loves us.

I remember as a child lingering at the Sunday dinner table, listening to guest ministers and missionaries tell of their work in churches and foreign countries. We listened, asked questions, and prayed with our guests.

The Legacy at the Table

Growing up, Sunday at noon was our biggest meal of the week. My mother cooked the best roast beef ever! God's bounty of fresh vegetables from the summer garden filled big bowls, and there would always be homemade devil's food chocolate cake for dessert. Or a freshly baked apple or peach pie. My mother taught me to bake using her chocolate cake recipe.[16]

She didn't have fancy china or crystal goblets. Our knives, forks, and spoons were stainless steel, and the plates and glasses didn't always match. Sometimes, a member of our family had a plate that was chipped.

Bob's parents entertained many people at their table, too. It was easy for our Russell family to follow suit. Although, not on a Sunday.

Giggles from the Back Seat

Since we ministered at a growing church with multiple services, it wasn't realistic for us to plan a big Sunday dinner at our house. It was late when church was over and the morning exhausted us. We would stop to eat and then head home to nap and rest.

I remember one particular Sunday we were trying to decide where to eat. We did our best to include the entire family in our decision. There were three choices: a restaurant, fast-food, or a buffet. That Sunday, the banter in the back seat became an unpleasant bickering session.

With his voice raised, which Bob seldom did, he said, "Okay! We are going to McDonald's for Chicken McNubbits. That's it!"

Dead silence! Chicken McNubbits? Then snickering from the back seat began welling up and whispering. Chicken McNubbits?

The boys said, "Dad, Chicken McNubbits?" We all burst out laughing. To this day, I want to call McDonald's Chicken Nuggets, Chicken McNubbits.

Yes, we ate in the car on the way home. Why? The Pittsburgh Steelers were playing football on TV. We didn't think ahead of time about taping the game.

That Sunday we could have picked up the Chicken McNubbits, gone home, laid them out, and gobbled them up fast! A quick meal, but around the table. Hmm. At least we prayed in the car.

Conversation Around the Table

We honeymooned in the Smoky Mountains more than 57 years ago. When the money we received as wedding gifts ran out, we headed home. We were there three nights and four days.

So, in May 2015, we went back and celebrated our 50th wedding anniversary. We took our boys and their families. It was perfect. Smoky Mountain National Park was a special place for all of us. We spent our summer vacations there when our two boys were grade-schoolers.

While our family sat around the table on that celebration night, one of our sons asked these questions. "Tell how you met and where was your first date? When did you first kiss Mom, Dad."

I doubt our kids would ask those questions had we not planned a special evening around the table.

Although that night someone else was the 'doer'. It was a special evening to laugh and reminisce about the past 50 years.

After our boys married and had children, they too realized it was important to have meals together as a family. Yes, it was hard. There were unending sports practices, games, meetings, church and school programs. One son's family was home-schooled, and he would come home and have lunch with them. Our other son is a police officer and sometimes worked the night shift. During that period, they ate an early breakfast together. Does it happen every day? No, but they did it several times a week.

I'm challenged to eat at the table with Bob, at least one meal a day. I'm not a morning person. So, our time is the dinner hour. I prefer eating at a table, not the kitchen counter or before the TV. And, I will set the table with place mats, napkins, dishes and silverware, even if we have carry-out for dinner that night.

How about a picnic in the park or dinner on your porch? Regardless of where we are, eating together at a table is the important thing. We need to keep those times unrushed and uninterrupted.

It is hard sometimes, but inviting people into our homes and asking them questions about their lives is priceless. Gathering around the table will bring you more joy than you can imagine. Let's all try it! It's hospitality at its finest!

> "Having a meal is more than eating and drinking. It is celebrating the gifts of life we share. A meal together is one of the most intimate and sacred human events. Around the table we become family, friends, community. Yes, a body."
> Henri Nouwen[17]

CHAPTER 9

Hunt and Gather for a Fuss-Free Dinner

"Whether you eat or drink or whatever you
do, do it all for the glory of God."

1 Corinthians 10:31, NIV

YOU SAID YES to hosting a group for a party. It was a sizeable
group, with little preparation and planning time allowed. And
you think, *why did I agree to this?*

Crammed for time can stress one out, sometimes to the
point of being ill. I've learned some shortcuts to ease those hours
of pressure while preparing for a successful gathering.

You want to do a home-cooked meal? Wonderful. But do a meal you love and have mastered in cooking.

I've cooked spaghetti and opened a can of sauce, but only one time did I cook an authentic Italian meal.

I was having lunch with my friend whose husband is from Italy. We talked about Italian cooking and doing an authentic Italian dinner. How fun it would be to do it with our dinner group that we were hosting in a few days.

The result of a successful dinner party, we hope, is not only great food but fun for everyone. Even for yourself.

When we finished lunch, I drove to an Italian food shop and purchased sauces and antipasto items and everything else I needed. I was going to cook an authentic Italian meal for our guests.

The night of our dinner we all stuffed ourselves with delicious, authentic Italian foods. Everyone enjoyed the meal.

The unexpected part of that evening meal was all the preparation and cleanup! Every dish and pan in my kitchen was dirty or in the dishwasher. It was midnight before everything was clean and I turned the lights out. Exhausted, I vowed to never do that dinner again.

Ah, changed my mind? The food was yummy, but the next time I will make adjustments. I can buy things from a deli and prepare some dishes ahead of time.

The result of a successful dinner party, we hope, is not only great food but fun for everyone. Even for yourself.

Friends call me *the hunter and gatherer.* And yes, I cook sometimes. Often, time is a premium and the older I get, the longer it takes. So, several years ago, I decided I needed to make some major adjustments when entertaining.

If you are hosting a party that needs food and desserts, look for places where food is prepared, ready for cooking, or catered.

Your grocery store has an assortment of foods you can buy. Do a taste test before you order.

A few years ago, I started ordering our Thanksgiving turkey dinner from a place that prepared things ahead of time, and I picked everything up on Wednesday afternoon. I love hosting that holiday dinner and now I'm not drop-dead tired before family arrives. I prepare favorite dishes a day or two earlier, as family traditions are important. So, we still fix corn pudding and pumpkin cake for our special day.

Here are examples of fresh meals I've ordered for our family and guests:

- Taco bar - Qdoba Mexican Eats.
- Baked potato bar - McAlister's Deli.
- Chicken - Chick-fil-A.
- Sub sandwiches - Sam's Club, Subway, etc.
- Pizza - Pizza Hut, Papa John's Pizza, etc.
- Italian - Olive Garden.
- Desserts - Nothing Bundt Cakes and other bakeries.
- Ice Cream - Graeter's Ice Cream, The Comfy Cow, grocery stores, etc.
- Ham dinner -The Honey Baked Ham Company, Boars Head ham from a deli.
- Barbecue - Momma's Mustard Pickles & BBQ, Mission Barbecue, or a favorite local barbecue restaurant in your city. Ours is Jucy's Barbecue.
- Soups and Entrée's - Cracker Barrel.
- Sweet Potato Casserole - Ruth's Chris Steak House.
- Thanksgiving dinner - Paul's Fruit Market, Kroger, or the grocery or market in your city.

- You want something quick some evening? Call your local delicatessen and ask what their entrées are that night. Order, and they will have things ready to be picked up.
- Wholesale stores such as Costco Wholesale or Sam's Club will carry most items you need for a party or dinner. The food items are ready to heat and serve.
- One of the first companies to offer meal kits was Omaha Steaks, founded in 1917. They began a mail order and home delivery service in 1952. We have used their wonderful products for years.
- Meal kits are pre-measured and ready for your family and guests. Recipes are healthy and nutritious, and there is no waste of food items. Just think of the time saved shopping. They have selections available that will not sacrifice your diet or health.

Entertaining is getting easier. Are you willing to try? When calculating the time, energy, and cost of many dishes for a large dinner, calling a caterer is appealing. It can be less money and waste. You don't have to cook an enormous fancy meal. Enjoy a laborious free day. Consider hunting and gathering ahead of time, though. The day before might prove disastrous. Yikes!

Have you ever gone online and ordered your groceries and picked up at your local grocery, curbside? That's a great time saver, too.

Check on restaurants that advertise a catering division. Order the food for your meal from them, especially if you need lots of food for lots of people. I order sweet potato casserole from Ruth's Chris Steak House for Thanksgiving. Their casserole beats my recipe I've used for years. No preparation for me. Plus, the cost is affordable and serves a crowd of twelve.

Our Kroger grocery stores have superb cranberry salad. I will buy a huge pan of the salad for Thanksgiving and Christmas. Check your local grocery store for items such as this for your family's holiday meal. It is unnecessary to labor the entire day before your holiday celebration or drag yourself out of bed bright and early and start cooking.

I don't want to discourage those of you who love to cook. Please continue doing so. For the others, hunt and gather. Remember, it is not the food on the table, but those seated on the chair.

Good Fairies Welcome

I wished someone would come and clean up the kitchen when we jumped up from the table and raced out of our house. Dirty dishes still on the table. Pots and pans in the sink. I used to say, "You think the good fairy will come?" I hated coming back to a messy kitchen.

After working at a convention all day, I dreaded going home, knowing everything would be in disarray with four extra houseguests. Exhausted, my mind and body needed rest.

I didn't look forward to walking into the kitchen that afternoon.

Oh my! Someone cleaned everything. Everything! The good fairy came!

The kitchen was spotless. Clean dishes in the dishwasher. Counters and table wiped clean. Trash can emptied. Scattered newspapers and magazines back in order. Carpet vacuumed, and wood floors shining.

Bob was to speak at the main session that night, and yet he helped me. I love him for that!

Okay-I don't believe in fairies. My sweet husband needed to get his mind off being nervous speaking before 25,000 people. And he was thinking about me!

CHAPTER 10

When It's Hard to Say Yes

"Above all, love each other deeply, because love
covers over a multitude of sins. Offer hospitality
to one another without grumbling."

1 Peter 4:8, 9, NIV

I LOOKED IN the mirror one afternoon thinking, 'why did I say yes to dinner at our house tonight?' I was tired and looked it. No blush or lipstick would be enough to cover the lines of dread as I faced the next few hours of preparation. I was thinking about how to cut corners, not hospitality!

I had to bite my tongue and say, I'm sorry Lord for grumbling. But I fall short sometimes.

Unexpected Guests on Derby Day

And they're off!

Every first Saturday of May, Louisville, KY is the center of worldwide attention. It's the Kentucky Derby horse race, and the most exciting two minutes in sports begins.

Unless you're a horse race lover, it's hard to understand the hoopla over the Kentucky Derby. It's a party-goer's day with all the elaborate hats, fancy dresses, colorful sport coats, food, fans, and Mint Juleps. For some of us, drinking a soda will suffice.

Most of the time we didn't want to battle the Derby Day crowd of partygoers and horse racing enthusiasts. We stayed home, skipped friends' parties, and watched the racing festivities on TV.

At about 9:00 o'clock Derby evening, the phone rang. A couple was driving home to Michigan. There was not a hotel room available within one hundred miles; did we know of a place? Their teenage daughter would be with them.

Bob hung up the phone and said, "Judy, we have company coming."

"Who are they?"

And Bob said, "I don't know."

"They're familiar with our church and saw the number in the phone directory. Did we know of someplace or someone who owned a bed-and-breakfast? I told them they are welcome to stay with us."

What just happened? I didn't understand.

"How soon will they be here?"

"In a half-hour."

"A half-hour?"

Thankfully, our extra room was clean. But it was Saturday night and late and, 'oh dear!'

We scrambled to put clean sheets on the hide-a-bed in the lower level of our home. A bath was across the hall. The teenage daughter will need to sleep on the living room sofa. That room would be private. We hurried to make beds and get extra towels. I touched up the bathroom; glad I always cleaned on Saturdays.

And then the doorbell rang.

We greeted our guests as they arrived. They looked exhausted after traveling all day from Florida.

We showed them to their rooms. Then gathered in our family room, talked and ate chocolate chip cookies and drank glasses of milk. Bob was familiar with their church in Michigan. Small world!

Suddenly tornado sirens wailed. Oh no! We didn't realize the city was expecting storms. Bob flipped on the weather channel and it showed a tornado just west of Louisville.

So off to the basement we headed. Gracious, our basement was not a very desirable place to camp out. It was unfinished, not too organized, lots of toys and games, a ping-pong table, and a train table.

We crawled under the train table, crouching together as we waited, sitting on a cold concrete floor. It was tight but safe quarters. Our two young sons and our dog Bandit, who feared storms, were all in the mix.

Imagine staring at complete strangers and wondering if a tornado would hit our house. We turned the TV volume up to listen to the weather report. I hate storms, but I trust God to protect his people.

Soon the sirens stopped, and the all-clear siren blew. It was safe to go upstairs.

Church was the next morning. I'm neither a breakfast maker nor an early riser, so cereal was the order of the day. Our overnight guests went to church with us and drove to their home in Michigan that afternoon. They were so appreciative and couldn't stop thanking us.

I've often thought of that evening. To have no room would be disheartening. Where would they have stayed? Would they have continued driving to Michigan? Have an accident?

We read in the book of Acts in the Bible about people walking miles and miles to the next city. No hotels, bed-and-breakfast inns or Airbnb's available. The traveler would find the home of a Christian, spend the night, and hopefully eat. That's why followers of Christ were instructed to practice hospitality.

That Derby Day night in May, we experienced a scene from Scripture. I was thankful we welcomed the traveling couple and their daughter to come and spend the night.

Several days later, a UPS truck delivered an enormous brown box from our weekend guests. It wasn't necessary to send us a thank you, but much appreciated. I called to tell them thank you and how much we will enjoy using those lovely towels. I have wondered, were our guests angels and we were unaware? One day, we might find out.

A Holy Terror Comes to Visit

I wasn't ready to say "hello", "welcome", or "make yourselves at home." I needed a hotel doorknob sign saying, "Do Not Disturb".

A couple we met several months earlier asked to come for the weekend. They were bringing their holy terror of a two-year-old son. How did I know he was a wild hare? I saw him in action when we met them. I would have to endure this family coming to our home for the weekend. My heart was not that of a joyful servant. Nope. I could think of nothing but me and my space as I grumbled under my breath.

The family arrived, and we showed them to their room. Before they even unpacked, their two-year-old was getting into everything: cabinets, toy boxes, opening and shutting doors, climbing on and jumping off furniture, flipping on and off the TV. Did anyone ever tell the child no?

On the last day of their visit, I heard banging on our piano. I couldn't believe my eyes; that holy terror of a boy was walking on the piano keys with his bare feet! Okay, now that's the straw that broke the camel's back!

I grabbed the boy in a flash and set him on the piano bench, spewing out a tongue lashing of serious words from this mother's mouth.

The shocked boy looked up at me wide-eyed. Did his parents ever tell him no? Mind you, it was a word he understood. The atmosphere was much calmer the last few hours they were in our home.

They left that afternoon. Praise God! Otherwise, I might have needed to lock myself in our bedroom before I did something more drastic.

I wondered what happened to those people? That undisciplined little boy? Did he grow up respecting his parents' authority and other people's property? I pray he did.

My heart was not right that weekend. I didn't want them, even though I worked at putting my best foot forward and a pretend smile on my face. It was fake, and I was not being honest.

Never hearing from them again, I wondered if the boy's mother overheard my words spoken to her son?

It's embarrassing to tell this. I do so because you may experience something similar or worse. I pray you don't experience family turmoil or upset guests of any age. That makes having the roast burn, the cream sauce scorch, the sink or toilet stop-up minor. Your life is not falling apart, it's just the sinful world we live in now.

Although it will be difficult, as the host, you must stay calm and show patience and kindness. And hope your guests will go away as happy as they came.

I felt guilty about the weekend. So, I sent them a brief note saying; "I hope your trip home was peaceful and safe."

That whole weekend wasn't a good experience for me. *I'm sorry, please forgive me, Lord, for grumbling and having a sorry attitude.*

CHAPTER 11

Lizards in Mombasa

"When you enter a house, first say, 'Peace to this house.'"

Luke 10:5, NIV

WE WALKED THE path towards our hotel room, intrigued with
the grounds and gardens. Colorful flowers, palm trees, and
tropical plants swayed in the breeze. A white sandy beach me-
andered along the Indian Ocean shoreline. We rounded the
corner. Groups of thatch-roofed huts loomed up, appearing to
be an African village.

The retreat for the African missionaries was being held at this
lovely seaside resort in Mombasa, Kenya. Missionaries traveled
from all over the continent for this special conference. Bob would
speak several times to those who served throughout Africa.

At this retreat, missionaries brought their children. This was a perfect vacation place to enjoy the pool and beach with volunteer adult supervisors while parents attended the sessions.

We discovered some unusual things about this part of Africa. Since the resort was near the Equator, the mornings were sultry. The afternoons and evenings would be much cooler and different from our home state of Kentucky.

At home, monkeys are at the zoo. But in Mombasa, we found baby monkeys, mommy monkeys, and daddy monkeys everywhere we turned.

Travel weary and thankful, my friend Jane, and I looked forward to some personal time and private space with our husbands.

Bob unlocked the door to our room. As we stepped inside, we found wooden floors, a cozy bedroom with queen beds, and lots of storage. And the nice-sized bathroom with a shower was a welcome discovery.

Someone delivered a welcome basket filled with huge bananas and oranges, a pineapple, and other kinds of fruit.

Gigantic windows opened in the resort's dining room. No screens for protection. You might as well kiss a banana goodbye if you are near the window and have one on your plate or in your hand. Monkeys would swing in the open window, grab it, and gobble it in one swallow. Watch out!

The time we spent with the missionary couples and their families was memorable. Each couple sacrificed to share the love of God with others; they deserved a special time of refreshing.

Our evening worship service uplifted everyone as we sang together and listened to Bob speak from God's word.

We walked to our room, and Bob unlocked the door. I stepped through the doorway, reached to flip on the light, and spotted a lizard-looking creature dart across the floor. It climbed up the bedspread, raced across the top, jumped off, and scaled the wall in a flash. And stopped. As if hanging in midair, our visitor clung to the wall, checking us out. Was he wondering what to do next?

To think of something slithering over us while we slept, made me shudder. That creepy thing has to go!

We tiptoed closer to the wall. Bob slipped his shoe off and began climbing up on the chair, trying to reach the unwanted intruder. It scurried along the ceiling's edge to the other corner.

Oh, my goodness. A hole about the size of my fist was in the room's corner. That's where the lizard disappeared. Now what? Does he live in that hole?

Years earlier, someone told me to stuff a mouse hole with aluminum foil. A mouse, supposedly, would not gnaw through the foil. True or not, I believed them. Will it work for a lizard? Let's hope so.

The fruit basket was lined with foil. As I began removing it, monkeys raced to our window, chattering and jumping. Did they see the fruit basket or hear the rattling sound of the foil? Smell the fruit?

I handed Bob the foil. He scrunched it up and began stuffing the foil into the hole. Perfect, it filled the hole.

I don't know where that lizard went, nor do I care. He was out of sight. I wondered if he would eat his way out through the foil. I hoped not. We never saw him again. Yay!

Yes, lizards fear us, and they eat the bugs. But I doubt you want one of those slithering creatures slinking around in your room or on your bed during the night? Not this resort guest!

I tried closing the windows to keep bugs out and who knows what else, but couldn't get them shut. We were open to the world of bugs, monkeys, and lizards.

I said to Bob, "Should we set the basket of fruit out on the patio table? I think the tantalizing odor is drawing creatures to our window."

We selected a few pieces of the fruit to eat later and I carried the basket outside to the patio table. I rushed back inside, shutting the door before monkeys could follow me. Remember? There are monkeys everywhere, lots of monkeys.

Within seconds, a bunch of them grabbed every piece of fruit, devouring it in one gulp.

Were they full enough now? I hoped so. I didn't want a monkey grabbing a banana from my hand at breakfast the next morning.

Should we tell our hosts? It wasn't their fault monkeys ate most of the fruit. Instead, we thanked them and expressed our appreciation for their thoughtful gesture of the fruit basket. We ate what we pulled out.

I was paranoid every time I opened the door of our room. I checked under the bed, glanced up the walls and over the ceiling. Thankfully, no lizards!

We enjoyed our talks with the missionaries at the conference. They appreciated the encouraging words and our thanking them for their service. The enthusiasm with which they served the people of Africa was refreshing. What a blessing to be a part of that group's retreat.

While we should always appreciate and be thankful for hospitality extended to us, we should be low-maintenance guests.

Unexpected things are bound to happen when one is a house guest or a hotel guest.

A guest crawls in bed and finds wet or dirty sheets or not enough blankets. Someone may have forgotten to put out clean towels, lay out a fresh bar of soap, or clean spider webs out of corners of the room. You may be hungry and have no food for a quick snack. Sometimes you have to speak with the hostess and ask for soap and towels or an unwanted creature crawls up the wall. Remember, look for the positive everywhere you visit.

Our visit was amazing, even though a lizard intruded our space. The whole time we were in Africa, we felt God's protection and care and we knew our family and church family were praying for good health and safety.

We will never forget the hospitality of each missionary. The time spent with them blessed us beyond measure.

Their uproarious and joyous laughter uplifted us as they shared story after story. The food we prepared and the food we tried was interesting. I never dreamed of eating Warthog stew! Or experiencing such unexpected things as monkeys stealing bananas out of your hand.

There were gorgeous sunrises, and the clear night sky full of countless twinkling stars was mesmerizing. There was no smog to cloud the stunning scenery. I will never forget the roaming wild animals on thousands of acres of land.

To experience a worship service outdoors with the Maasai congregation was unusual. To have an interpreter relaying Bob's message was touching. The songs sang, scriptures read, and prayers given uplifted us even though we didn't understand a word. It was the expression on their faces and the tones coming from their voices; you knew they loved Jesus.

CHAPTER 12

Big Parties

"The King will reply, 'Truly I tell you, whatever you did for one of
the least of these brothers and sisters of mine, you did for me.'"

Matthew 25:40, NIV

IN OUR 50-PLUS years of ministry, we often invited big groups to
our home for parties. Parties can be lots of work, but they're
fun and open doors to building deeper friendships. Big parties
do not have to be expensive, either.

Holidays like Christmas, Easter, the first day of summer,
or Halloween can be perfect times for big parties, and guys
love gathering for sporting event parties such as the Super
Bowl.

Next Door Neighbors

Months in advance, I put the date on the calendar. Spring is bursting into vivid colors with white flowering pear trees, redbud trees, yellow daffodils, and white and pink dogwoods. We always invited our neighbors to our church Easter Pageant and to our house afterwards for dessert. It had become a tradition we looked forward to.

Neighbors began asking about it early in the year. Those evenings often lasted past midnight. I realized we were the key to the length of the fellowship time. We needed to encourage discussions and make the evening fun and interesting for our guests, not hoping they would hurry to eat and go home.

We all enjoyed those evenings; no one ever missed. I look back on those years as treasured memories around our table. It was a time when we grew closer to our neighbors. A few times we did a catered dinner or a potluck dinner. Other times, we had dessert.

Neighborhood Open House

After we moved to our condo, we needed a reason to meet our new neighbors. An open house would be perfect. It was time for a party.

I love planning and organizing for a get-together. Searching and coming up with ideas for parties is fun. I might have been a party planner had I not married a preacher.

A pretty fall design on the four-by-six-inch card was ideal for the open house invitation. It included the who, what, when, where and why along with the RSVP. The online company Shutterfly.com printed them.

Friends in the neighborhood said they wanted to help. So, my friend Susan and I hand-addressed each envelope. Her husband Mike put them in each mailbox one evening and I alerted everyone by email there was a note in their mailbox.

The yes replies started coming in from our new neighbors. A few declines, and why they couldn't attend. That tells me they wanted to come. People were getting excited. Me too.

I browsed Pinterest for ideas for fall parties. Oh my, what an addiction that site could become. When I searched apple cider and donuts, bunches of pins popped up on the page. These days, lots of brides are serving donuts at their wedding receptions. My mind began spinning and dreaming as I saw ideas.

I asked Susan if her son could make some donut stands with dowel rods, to stack donuts for self-serving. I emailed several ideas to him. He said the stand needed to be a much larger round base and have three spindles at various heights attached to hold the donuts. A smaller one could easily be knocked onto the counter.

So, he made a large one, twelve inches in diameter, with three spindles at various heights. He painted it grey, and it was perfect as we stacked three dozen donuts on that stand.

Donut holes on wooden skewers stood tall in a cut-glass ice bucket. I stacked donuts in a tiered shape on a pedestal cake stand. Eyelet paper doilies separated each donut, so they didn't stick to one another.

I found footed glass coffee mugs for hot apple cider, less than $2 each. What did we do before Amazon.com?

There is a fruit and vegetable farm across the Ohio River in southern Indiana. People in this part of the country will drive there to buy Huber's Apple Cider. It is the best apple cider anywhere and on my list of favorite foods.

I borrowed three hot-drink pump dispensers from another neighbor up the street. They were perfect for serving Huber's Apple Cider. And you've got to serve world-famous Krispy Kreme donuts if you have hot apple cider from Huber's. As I'm writing, I'm salivating over their yummy pumpkin donuts. Perfect for fall parties.

I wrote the kinds of donuts on ceramic place cards. By

placing them at the base of each donut-stacked dowel rod, people could decide which kind they wanted to try first.

We laid out cinnamon sticks to use as stirrers for the cider, if guests desired. Salted mixed nuts were in bowls placed around the room. Nuts help balance out the sweetness of the donuts. Beverage sized rust-colored napkins were perfect for holding a donut. No need for plates.

Fresh fall flowers were on the tables, mums on the porch, a welcome sign on the front step, and a big fall wreath on the front door. LED candles in silver lanterns throughout our home gave a golden glow for a warm fall welcome.

I found name tags with gold-colored edging in a shop, perfect for a fall open house. We wrote the names of every guest who said yes, along with their street address on a name tag. And placed them in alphabetical order on the credenza at the front door.

You may wonder why their street address? I thought remembering guests by their name and street name would help us place them on one of the four streets in our neighborhood. It helped me.

The open house was from 7:00-8:30 p.m. Everyone came at 7:00 p.m. sharp! I'm sure they were wondering what they might find in this preacher's home. How would we greet them? Will they have an enjoyable time? With our home being so open, we hosted forty-five people that evening. It made a delightful and fun night to get acquainted with our new neighbors.

Yes, it took effort and work to plan and prepare for the open house. Whenever we do something worthwhile, it always takes effort.

Not everything will be perfect. While talking with a couple ladies, I spotted something grey sticking off the edge of the tall white bookcase. Only to discover it was a home-made paper airplane our grandsons had been flying. You just have to laugh—even about a paper airplane.

I think back on that evening and remember laughter and getting acquainted with wonderful new friends.

We greet them as they are taking walks in the neighborhood. Several of us met and watched the eclipse together. We have one neighbor that gathers several folks' garbage cans and pushes them up to their garage doors after trash day pickup. This loving neighborhood cares about each other. They watch out for each other. Several attend our church. What a blessing to live here.

We received kind notes and emails thanking us for opening our home. What a joy to say we care about you, even though we just met.

Ice Cream Party

One spring, we hosted an unusual neighborhood party at our home—a concert by Christian storytellers and singers, Steve and Annie Chapman. The hour-long concert of touching stories with songs of life and family inspired everyone.

Guess what we served our guests? Graeter's Ice Cream Sundaes! Who doesn't love ice cream? This was the perfect summer party dessert.

Consider getting ice cream for your next summer party. We set out plastic glasses for sodas and water along with a bucket of ice. Graeter's delivered assorted choices of ice cream. Scoops of chocolate, vanilla, butter pecan and raspberry chocolate chip were in individual-sized round cups with lids and packed in dry ice.

We put fresh strawberries in strawberry sauce and added chocolate and caramel sauce in serving dishes so guests could spoon a sauce over their ice cream. Chopped pecans and delicious bright juicy red Maraschino cherries were available to top the sundaes. Oh yes, there was yummy homemade whipped cream, too! Simple, delicious, and so much fun. Everyone loved that dessert.

Waffle Bar Party

For a summer evening dessert, serve waffles with assorted ice cream and syrups. I love the possibilities of a waffle party.

Nothing is worse than soggy waffles. Prepare waffle mix and cook in waffle pan. To keep them crisp, lay waffles on a cooling rack placed on a baking sheet. Stick in an oven, uncovered, at 200 degrees.

Here are some ideas for waffle toppings: Sliced bananas and strawberries, blueberries and raspberries, blackberries and cherries, cinnamon apples, roasted pears, grilled pineapple, chocolate chips, crushed nuts, softened butter, powered sugar and more. Include assorted syrups and plenty of whipped cream.

If serving waffles for a brunch, add assorted juices along with ham, bacon, sausage or fried chicken.

Coffee Bar Party

Host a coffee party. People who love coffee will enjoy making different concoctions.

Select different coffees, creamers, and syrups—chocolate, vanilla, strawberry, raspberry, and caramel. Set out mix for hot cocoa and add whipped cream, in case someone wants hot chocolate instead. Don't forget sugar and honey and spices, such as cinnamon, nutmeg, and pumpkin pie spice.

Family Reunions

On July 10th, every year, a vast group of relatives gathered for the annual Kehl family reunion and celebration of my grandfather's birthday. It was fun being with cousins, aunts, and uncles we seldom saw.

Why a reunion? We need to schedule spending time with people we love. Otherwise, it will never happen. People are just too busy.

Often, the Kehl reunion was at my parents' home. People were scattered throughout the house and out in the yard. Everyone brought a dish to share.

Our family cleaned and worked in the yard to make everything lovely. My mother would bake her Devils' food cake and fix fruit Jell-O, as they were always in demand. Even if we went to someone else's house, they expected her to bring both.

Every year at Thanksgiving, my dad's family gathered. His brothers and sister and cousins would all come to our house or one of his brothers.

The Thomas reunion wasn't as large as the Kehl reunion. Since November was a winter month, people gathered in the house. Men watched football games while ladies talked and busied themselves in the kitchen, preparing the meal of the year!

When I got older, I washed the dishes after our Thanksgiving dinner. My aunts and cousins couldn't keep up with me. It was fun racing to see how fast we could finish! They enjoyed talking and were not in a hurry to clean the kitchen. Don't ask me why they never used paper cups and plates! And plastic silverware? I'm not sure plastic forks were very prevalent then.

I hated when they handed me the pots and pans. Yuck! Pots and pans are hard to wash. Another question? In order to soak away the food particles ahead of time, why didn't they fill the pans with water? Ah, yes, I remember. That would waste water.

We still gather some years with my brother and sister and our family. A time of glorious memories.

To gather for a picnic was one of Bob's mother's favorite things to do. The Russell family used to meet at a Kentucky or Indiana State Park for a day in the early summer.

The grandkids went swimming, everyone played games, and there was always lots of family talk, laughter, and eating.

Now we meet every couple of years for several days of reunion time.

Reunions offer the opportunity to reconnect, reminisce and enjoy each other's company. It is a perfect time for taking photos and making memories.

Cruise trips and destination trips at a resort can be very expensive. When planning for family events and budgets, remember who will be attending. It doesn't have to be extravagant.

On the next page, I've listed tips for planning a reunion and several websites to help you get started.

Yes, it's work. There are days you will be excited and days you want to pull your hair out. But remember, all your hard work will make a memorable event for the family. You think someone will volunteer to plan it the next time?

How to Plan and Organize a Simple Family Reunion

1. Start planning a year in advance: when, where, and how many days. Form a small committee and ask for help with ideas and details.
2. Gather emails, cell phone numbers, and mailing addresses to reconnect with family members.
3. Create a Facebook page for updates and keeping connected.
4. Get a headcount, two to three weeks prior, of those planning on attending.
5. Book a hotel and ask for group rates. Ask each family to book their own reservation.
6. Plan a budget. Consider the cost per person to cover the expenses of paper plates, soft drinks, ice, a catered meal, etc.
7. Decide about meals. Will they be potluck, catered, carried out from a restaurant, or a bar dinner, such as hamburgers, hotdogs, tacos, or an ice cream bar and toppings? A serve-yourself meal? Consider planning simple and inexpensive meals, as some families can't always afford a lavish dinner out.
8. Consider having families pay for most meals ahead of time as a deposit to confirm they will be coming. Announce the last date of deposit so each family can save their money.
9. Open a bank account for monies collected from deposits and other fees. This will make it easier to keep the funds separate from the planner's own personal account.
10. Have each family bring their favorite board game.
11. Ask family members to take photos and post on the personal group Facebook page.
12. Enjoy your family reunion.

Take a look at these articles for additional ideas:
moneycrashers.com/tips-plan-family-reunion-budget/family-treemagazine.com/reunions/10-steps-to-family-reunion-success/

CHAPTER 13

Ditching the Me Syndrome

"Do nothing out of selfish ambition or vain conceit. Rather, in humility value others above yourselves, not looking to your own interests but each of you to the interests of the others."

Philippians 2:3, 4, NIV

ONE EVENING BOB said, "I invited someone to come over next Sunday night for chili, is that okay?" Uh, thinking, 'I have Sweet Spirit Singers rehearsal on Sunday nights, and I'm the director,' as I swung around and "Grrr" under my breath. And then Satan and I argued.

Rehearsal is over at 6:30 p.m. Things could be ready before I left for rehearsal, but I am too tired on Sunday afternoons. That "me" syndrome was wedging its way into my thinking again.

I was overlooking the fact that on Saturday afternoon I could prepare a simple pot of chili. Oh, but the boys have basketball games, right?

By Saturday night, I want the laundry completed, the beds remade with clean sheets, and the carpet swept. The 'ole devil planted thoughts in my mind. Thoughts such as 'you can't', 'you don't have time', 'you don't measure up', or 'your budget will be tight that week'. It becomes about me, not the person invited to grace our home. But me. We allow those ridiculous and horrible thoughts to hammer at us. I was being disrespectful to my husband and God and forgetting the Scripture that calls us to be hospitable.

When was the last time you and your family entertained? In our fast-paced and digital world, entertaining is rare.

Preachers who grace our table have expressed that they never get invited by families from their church for dinner or dessert. Or worse yet, my wife has no friends.

That breaks my heart. I hesitate a moment, considering how can I respond to this?

If you want friends, be a friend. To get an invitation to someone's home, welcome people into your home.

That response may sound harsh, but I believe it's true.

Why not text someone and ask if they are free to come to lunch next Thursday? Make the meal simple. Serve tuna sandwiches or grilled cheese and heat a can of soup or fix a big salad.[18]

You might call or email a couple and invite them to dinner. Prepare chili or hamburgers or order pizza or pick up food at a deli. Chances are the invited guests will ask if they can help and bring a pie or a fresh salad. People want to do something. Let them. Enjoy your evening together.

Oh yes, arrange your schedule to include a brief nap before guests arrive.

In her popular book *Bread and Wine*,[19] Shauna Niequist

proclaims "fuss not". Chuck perfectionism out the window. She used the illustration that her mother never set a jar of jelly on the table. She always presented it in a crystal bowl and silver spoon ready.

I can fit between those two examples: Fuss not or perfect. Sometimes I do simple and sometimes more perfect. Please know it can never be perfect. The older and slower I get, the less perfectionism on my part. If you are a young married couple, remember, things will not be perfect.

Although, when I use plastic plates, cups, and utensils, I enjoy placing a real tablecloth on the table with big paper napkins. I prefer fresh flowers. When we arrange a vase of flowers along with candles on the table, we are telling our guests they are special. I may put bread on a plate and butter in a nice dish and potato chips in a bowl.

If we are rushing at lunchtime, and it's just Bob and me, I might lay an open chip bag on the table. Far from perfection.

I continue to remind myself that the devil is doing his best to destroy my joy and make me miserable. Will you join me in telling him to get out and leave us alone?

We are to be hospitable. Before guests arrive, why not pray and invite our Lord and Savior to be part of the guest list?

CHAPTER 14

Easter Matters

"For God so loved the world that he gave his one and only Son,
that whoever believes in him shall not perish but have eternal life."

John 3:16, NIV

PEOPLE REMEMBER MOMENTS. It's a phone call, a note, an invitation, time together. Ask people their favorite memories and they're often simple: fishing with dad, ice cream cones on the porch, sports games, warm cookies, picnics, and always holidays. Dyeing Easter eggs is always a fun time to gather with family or friends.

The phone rang. My niece and her family were close. They

wanted to stop for the afternoon. We seldom see them, and I was excited about this unexpected visit.

Since it was near Easter, I thought it would be fun to decorate Easter eggs. I boiled eggs and set up egg coloring supplies on our kitchen table.

Over the years, we've dyed eggs with lots of different people. We did traditional egg dyeing with our boys when they were small and with our grandchildren. We tried different egg coloring techniques through the years. College students home on spring break and young moms and preachers' wives have come and colored eggs at our house.

I took a Pysanka egg coloring class with a friend. We loved it, even though it was harder and more time-consuming. To start, we blew the yoke out of the egg. Then we drizzled hot wax on the shell in a design that would eventually be filled with dye. The pattern was very intricate and beautiful. It was not a simple task and too difficult for children.

My favorite way to dye eggs is with silk ties or scarves. It will surprise you how they turn out as sometimes it's a mystery. The dyed egg may look different from the original design on the tie or scarf. Supplies needed for more quick and traditional egg coloring are available in craft stores, grocery stores, and drugstores.

Here are several ways to try decorating eggs at Easter time.

The Silk Method

Use old ties and scarves from your closet. They must be silk for this project. Thrift stores have silk ties and scarves you can buy if you need extra supplies.

Cut squares from the silk large enough to pull up around the egg.

Position the colorful side of the fabric against the egg. Use a twist tie to hold material taunt.

The colors will be brighter if you use pieces of white material from an old sheet or pillowcase and wrap around the egg on top of the silk piece. This will help keep water from getting directly on the egg.

Place the eggs in a large pan filled with water two inches above the eggs. Add 1/4 cup of vinegar.

Boil the water and let simmer for twenty minutes.

Remove the wrapped eggs with tongs, placing them on paper towels.

Let the eggs cool to room temperature. Waiting is no fun, but necessary!

Invite everyone to gather around the table for snacks and sodas while you wait. A perfect time for fun and fellowship with family and friends.

When eggs have cooled, gently remove the fabric wrappings.

Store in the refrigerator until ready to display.

Rub with vegetable oil for a shine.

The Traditional Fashion

This was how I learned to color eggs for Easter using food coloring.

Add about 25 drops of food coloring to 1/2 cup warm water placed in a glass or bowl, deep enough for water to cover the egg. Place an egg in the colored water for a few moments.

Remove the egg with a teaspoon when it reaches the desired color. Place it on an empty egg carton turned upside down to dry.

Rub them lightly with vegetable oil once the dye is dry for a shine.

Decorating Ideas Using Easter Eggs

Lay the eggs in a small crystal bowl or basket and set it on your table as a centerpiece. I'm sure your china cabinet has some interesting glass bowls or hurricane globes that can be filled with the eggs.

An egg can be a place card at your Easter dinner table. A person's name written on the egg in calligraphy will look lovely.

One decorated egg placed in a bird's nest from a craft store will make a great favor or place card. You could attach a piece of ribbon with glue to the nest and add a person's name down the length of the ribbon.

Note in chapter 32 doing Resurrection Easter eggs with grandchildren.

CHAPTER 15

New Bride's Dishes for Setting the Table

"Blessed are those who are invited to the
wedding supper of the lamb."

Revelation 19:9, NIV

I WAS PINCHING pennies in college when my roommate told me
about going to an on-campus meeting to hear a china salesperson speak. Mind you, Bob and I were dating, but not engaged.
I was clueless about dishes and whether I wanted fancy, plain,
or nothing.

As you might guess, I bought fine china and made payments for many months. The plates were white with a classic platinum silver border and are still a dining room staple in our home. I could only afford eight place settings: dinner plates, salad plates, cups and saucers, and two different sizes of meat platters.

The shipment arrived, and I was about to pop as I ripped open the box. Anxious about my decision, I unpacked the dishes and displayed them on my desk, wanting my friends to see. After they oohed and aahed over my choice, I packed everything back in the box and tucked it in my closet for the future, thinking I didn't need to add eight place settings of fine dishes to a wedding registry.

According to the online wedding gift registry, zola.com, one-third of today's brides will select place settings of fine china for their new home. Not just everyday dishes, but place settings of classic fine bone china, and often in white. Others may choose a more casual style in white.

Are people inspired when they sit at your table?

When my granddaughters were young, they started asking, "Nana, can we set the table fancy tonight?" I loved hearing those words!

So, my granddaughters and I set the table fancy.

I pulled out my fine white fancy china. Over the years, I discovered adding seasonal salad plates or dessert plates, along with flowers, napkins, and other accents helped to keep the white plates looking fresh and new. These additions added to the fun of setting an interesting table.

I have collected unique patterns of salad and dessert plates for years. It's less expensive than buying a new set of dishes for every holiday or occasion. Colorful plate chargers add a whole new dimension to your place setting as well.

My daughters-in-law worried I might develop an addiction to plate shopping! I reasoned with them that my granddaughters could divide the dishes up with each other when they get married, providing they still want them.

> "When a guest sits down, there should be something beautiful and inspiring to see."
> Annie Falk, author of *Palm Beach Entertaining*[20]

Set a Pretty Table

It may be hard for gals to set a fancy table when first married; especially if fancy doesn't fit their lifestyle. Here are a few ideas to help get you started with your table setting, along with thoughts I've gleaned from bloggers Kelley Nan[21] and Sandy Coughlin.[22]

1. Consider eight white dinner plates.

   Work to complete at least 12 four-piece place settings. First dinner plates, then salad plates. After those two basic components, add cups and saucers. White salad plates can be every day luncheon plates. Over time, increase your china collection with other pieces, such as bread and butter plates and bowls.

   Think about asking your mother or family members for extra china or serving pieces for a birthday or Christmas gift. My Mother helped me with those extra pieces. One year I received a gravy boat that matched my china pattern and another year, stemmed goblets. I gave my daughter-in-law plates that matched her Christmas china.

2. Be thoughtful about table linens.

   Begin with one dozen no-iron napkins in white and one large no-iron white tablecloth. Extra napkins can wrap hot rolls in a bowl to place on the table.

There were times I needed to use my imagination to create an unusual table scape. So, I pulled out a white or plain colored twin sheet as a substitute tablecloth. Tied a ribbon around the sheet at each table leg to keep the sheet from dragging on the floor. Then I puffed the corners by pulling the sheet up above the ribbon.

3. Add color to place settings by tying satin ribbons around the folded napkins.

I love satin floppy bows in seasonal colors. There is no need to buy multiple sets of napkin rings. Instead, buy spools of 1½ inch wide ribbon found at a craft store and cut pieces sixteen inches or more in length. Tie the ribbon around the folded napkin and let the extra ribbon dangle on the table. Instant color.

Ribbon storage is minimal. Just roll up and paper clip one side of the roll and slip the ribbon into a zip-lock bag.

4. Skip stemmed goblets.

Choose stemless glasses that hold ten to twelve ounces of water or tea. If you are adamant about stemmed goblets, search for heavy ones that can withstand use by a variety of guests. Use them often. Buy more costly crystal stemmed goblets later.

5. Choose a timeless piece of china that can substitute for different things.

A timeless piece such as a soup tureen can be a wise investment. On one occasion serve soup from the tureen to your guests. Next time use it as a vase for a floral centerpiece, either on the dining room table or buffet. Timeless pieces can be conversation starters, too.

6. A glass ice bucket

The ice bucket can be for chilled beverage bottles or ice, or used as a vase for roses.

7. Have two glass pitchers or an inexpensive glass carafe.

This is the perfect piece for pouring beverages. A large pitcher for tea or lemonade, and a smaller pitcher for water or juice. Either will be a nice accessory sitting on an open shelf or used as a vase.

8. A small and large white platter.

A platter is handy for serving hors d'oeuvres, meats, bread, brownies, etc. They are useful as veggie trays or carrying hamburgers or steaks from the grill. Use as a decorative piece by leaning on a shelf or kitchen counter.

9. Choose 10 or 12 place settings of flatware.

If you choose only eight sets, your chances of running out are greater. I suggest a simple classic flatware design in quality stainless steel. Remember to count the pieces when you are emptying the dishwasher. Many times, a spoon or fork disappear and end up in the trash can. Yes, go digging for it!

10. You will need quality food containers.

Choose ones that will take you from refrigerator to oven, then table. I still have and use Corning Ware casserole dishes I received 57 years ago for wedding gifts. Those kinds of containers are smart investments. You can use them for serving vegetables, salads, or fruit. Consider getting white to compliment other colors.

11. Use a gravy boat as an extra serving dish.

This smaller dish is perfect for holding foods served at the table such as cranberry sauce or applesauce or as a candy dish. You can display it on a shelf, too.

12. Add candle holders and candles.

Nothing says fancy table better than candles and flowers. I love LED candles. I've collected them over the past several years. They have a timer I set to come on every evening at 5:30 p.m. They go off at about 11:30 p.m. I love the ambiance of candles glowing. Always keep a stash of batteries handy.

Candles, candlestick holders, pillar candles, and lanterns are rare wedding gifts. I love giving them to a bride and groom. I enjoy choosing something unique and different as a surprise. And a thoughtful candle gift may be the only one the couple receives.

Three silver-plated or three brass candlesticks make a great bridal shower gift. Buy them in a variety of heights from a reputable store. Get timed LED candles that fit the candlesticks. The bride will love them. They look great grouped together in a variety of places such as the dining room table, hall table, buffet, or mantle. The bride can add a pair of classic crystal candlestick holders later.

Try the candle in the holder you are purchasing, as candles may not fit some candlestick holes. It could be an embarrassing evening if someone hits the table leg and the candle taper falls out on the table or worse, drops on your guest's plate of food. To avoid worrying if that will happen, select a candlestick with deep holes.

A lantern holding a pillar candle and placed on the dining room table is striking. Add some fresh flowers and a garland of eucalyptus greenery. Dramatic!

I enjoy a lantern or a grouping of them lit and set on a table, the mantle, a shelf, counter, or in a corner. It adds a homey, warm touch to the room.

Most of all, enjoy setting your table and blessing guests with genuine hospitality.

How to Set a Place Setting

Today, most hostesses entertain more casually than formally. I do casual, with a hint of formal.

At a casual gathering, position a placemat on the table in front of each chair. Use a tablecloth for more formal gatherings. Let it hang six inches off the edge of the table. You don't want the cloth dragging across a person's lap.

Some people lay placemats on the tablecloth or they use a charger. Both give added color and dimension to the place setting.

The plate goes in the center of the placemat, with the left edge hanging over the right side of the napkin.

Next, one consideration is to place the napkin on the left side of the placemat or charger. Cloth napkins are preferred. Fold in half or fourths. You could also position the napkin across the middle of the plate, or as many restaurants do, put it in a glass.

Some suggest placing the napkin to the left of the forks rather than under them. The napkin is the first item picked up by guests; and often forks drop off and are noisy. My preference is to place the forks on the napkin, particularly when seating is tight around your table. At more formal events, place napkins across guests' plates. This is a good time to use napkin rings.

Place forks on a napkin in order of when they are being used. Beginning from the far left, a salad fork is first and then a dinner fork next to the plate. Fork prongs are to be pointed upwards, towards the middle of the table.

On the right side of the plate is a knife, with the serrated edge facing towards the plate. Next is a teaspoon. If serving soup, place the soup spoon to the right of the teaspoon. Check out Chapter 38 for a simple trick for how to remember where the fork, knife, and spoon are placed.

Depending on the dessert being served, place a fork at the

top of the plate with prongs pointing to the left. If using a spoon, place it above the fork and the bowl of the spoon facing left.

Now, where are the glasses placed? The water glass goes just off the placemat at top of the knife. If using a second glass, place it on the top right corner of the placemat.

The bread & butter plate is positioned at the top left of each dinner plate with a small butter knife laying across the top of the plate.

When a more formal gathering, salad plates are placed on top of dinner plates. If salad is served with the meal, place the salad plate to the top left of the forks. Move the bread & butter plate above the forks, closer to the dessert fork and spoon.

If your main course is a salad, place it in individual bowls. But, when serving salad with the meal, the serving is smaller and can be put on a salad plate.

The coffee or teacup can be brought to the table with dessert. Set cups below the glasses and to the right.

Add place cards above the dessert spoons at the top of the plate. They can also be positioned on top of the napkin that is on the plate. If most of the guests are unknown to each other, add their name on the front and back of the place card. Guests around the table can see the name of whom they are speaking with from across the table.

Flowers, potted plants, candles, lanterns, and vases are perfect items to use as centerpieces on your table.

Enjoy setting a lovely table.

CHAPTER 16

Christmas Matters

"The angel said to them, 'Do not be afraid. I bring you good news
that will cause great joy for all the people. Today in the town of
David a Savior has been born to you; he is the Messiah, the Lord.'"

Luke 2:10, 11, NIV

THE FIRST SIX months that we lived in Louisville, church people
invited us for dinners and parties. I wondered if I could be as
cordial and considerate and hospitable.

So, we took our turn and signed up to host the Sunday
school class Christmas party. This was a new experience for us,
hosting a Christmas party with ten couples.

As the date grew closer, my priorities were out of order. To clean a two-bedroom apartment and prepare food while four months pregnant should not be that big an issue. Ah, but it developed into one. The issue? Me!

I thought I would straighten up the cabinets in the kitchen and wash off the stovetop and refrigerator shelves. Oh yes, the bathroom vanity, the tub, and the commode need cleaning. The floors need mopping and polishing. I should reorganize our dresser drawers and spruce up the closets. Polish the furniture and decorate for Christmas, and ... and ....

Wait. What was I thinking?

What do we serve the guests? Don't they serve caviar at parties in Louisville and other fancy hors d'oeuvres?

We need fresh-baked cookies, homemade chocolate fudge, and tiny ham sandwiches at least. Isn't that expected? How do I prepare for everything? This will blow our budget.

I stood in our closet an hour before the party was to start. Mad and crying. I didn't want to host this party. I wanted to lock the door, turn off the lights and crawl into bed. I was not ready for guests. Bob calmed me down and helped to finish up the preparations just as the doorbell rang.

Later in the evening, I stood for a moment and watched our guests as they enjoyed the party. The food was tasty and Christmas decorations sparkled on the tree.

I realized that if I prepared for company and made everything perfect, I was forgetting the most important part of the evening—the people! I am thankful that Bob could see the big picture and helped me see it too.

It's a reminder that, if I am not careful, Satan will plant negative thoughts in my mind, and I will miss those wonderful times.

College Cookie Decorating Party

I was adamant college students would love decorating Christmas cookies. Our college minister argued they would be bored. When college kids arrive home the week of Christmas, they are looking for an opportunity to party.

I collected cookie cutters for years. They would work perfectly for this party.

All afternoon I baked cookies. The aroma of dozens of baked sugar cookies permeated our house. It was the smell of Christmas everyone loves.

There were many large and small cookie cutters available with a variety of designs. Some students were artistic and enjoyed doing the big ones and others would venture only with the small ones.

The cookies were ready to decorate. Food coloring mixed with powdered sugar makes a basic icing in red, blue, green, yellow, etc. The icing was now ready along with toothpicks, spatulas, knives, and spoons.

We would use none of the fancy disposable decorating bags and tips. Kids needed to be imaginative and spend time on just one cookie. Simple decorating supplies it would be. Oh yes, and several rolls of paper towels for laying their work on and using for cleanup.

Over twenty college-aged kids came, and I can't tell you how many said I've never decorated cookies before this. It shocked me!

Talk about a successful student party. They laughed and teased each other as they took turns decorating. The kitchen table couldn't hold everyone at the same time. Six or eight rather reluctantly took their turn as they began creating a masterpiece, while others oohed and giggled.

They needed an incentive to do their best. We told them ahead of time about prizes for the best decorated, the ugliest, the prettiest, the most artistic, to spur them on in their project.

That first year, as we judged the cookies, I thought, 'let's save the winner, loser, and other prize-winning cookies and show them the next year'. An airtight container worked to keep the cookies and pull out the following year.

I sensed we would host this party again. Perhaps winners would improve their skills, and they did. To see last year's creations, poking fun and teasing, stirred their interest to decorate again.

Some cookies from that first year appeared as works of art. Some ... uh ... looked sad. The Christmas cookie decorating party at Bob and Judy's became a yearly event for many years. I wish you could have seen the major improvement in students decorating skills.

What do you think? Would you host a Christmas cookie decorating party for your church's college students? It is lots of fun.

Reuben the Shepherd Pays a Visit

In mid-December, our son Phil and his family and mutual friends were coming to dinner for the evening. Holly and her girls babysat our grandchildren, and we wanted their family to come, too.

The specific time scheduled for the surprise visitor was getting close, and no one knew about the guest except me.

Grandchildren were fidgety, wanting to play in the other room.

We seldom leave our table quickly, as the flow of a conversation will change when people move. This was different. It was time for my surprise visitor to open the door.

I said, "Let's go to the family room."

Bob looked at me, puzzled as I glared at him, wanting this to be a surprise.

People offered to help gather dishes and take them to the kitchen. I turned the dining room light off.

The surprise visitor waited patiently outside in the cold weather for a signal showing we were ready. Dimmed dining room lights, unlocked porch door. It was time.

Christmas tree lights were twinkling, the fireplace crackling and candles flickering in the shadows. Family and guests made themselves comfortable.

Phil and his three children were sitting on the floor close by the door. Perfect spot, or so I thought!

The back door opened, and a sandaled foot appeared. Phil, a police sergeant, grabbed for his gun. People's eyes popped wide and jaws dropped in startled silence.

Who invited this stranger to come unannounced, and without a polite knock?

Bob gave me that questioning look again. Our youngest grandchild clung to his dad.

The surprise guest said, "I'm Reuben the shepherd, and a baby boy has been born in the city of Bethlehem. Heavenly angels sang, and shepherds left their flocks of sheep on the hillside to go visit the baby. Wise men came to see the child. It is the long-predicted Savior, Christ the Lord, and his name is Jesus."

Chapman cowered up to his dad. This was an unusual sight at Nana and Pop's house.

By now, our older guests were settling into the story and the grandchildren inched closer, wondering, is this real?

They listened intently as Reuben the Shepherd finished telling the Christmas story. He began asking questions. Had they listened? Would they have the right answer?

There were a few uncomfortable seconds that passed before seven-year-old Andy quipped,

"Why are you wearing that watch and ring?"

Despite his efforts to be authentic, Reuben forgot to remove his watch and wedding ring. We all laughed and Reuben and

Bob began bantering back and forth, only as genuine friends could do. As unexpected as he walked in, Reuben the Shepherd walked out.

Sometimes it's fun to surprise guests at a dinner party. It takes detailed and advanced planning, and I should have warned Bob and Phil. I hadn't planned on Officer Phil Russell pulling his gun. Oops!

Later, Holly commented. "I remember how relaxing and fun the evening was. Your home is warm and welcoming and it was a delightful treat to have Reuben visit after dinner. My kids still talk about it. The most important thing to me was that you made us feel comfortable in your home!"

It's Just a Sofa

We were ready, but not for what happened next. The candles were lit and the wreaths hung, the trees decorated and their lights glowing. Food was on the table, and it was time for our church's senior adults, who were members of the Sixty Club, to celebrate their annual Christmas party. We were hosting and expected a fun evening.

People arriving were excited, laughing, and greeting and hugging each other as we hung coats in the closet. Each lady was dressed in her Christmas party attire and their husbands wore coats and ties. Everyone was excited.

We served assorted cookies and candies along with the usual Christmas party foods and a punch. The menu was perfect. I placed red napkins and plates on the table, and the tasty party punch was ready. I made it with ginger ale, pineapple juice, and Hawaiian punch—perfect for Christmas, refreshing and colorful.

We moved furniture around in the living room and brought in other chairs to accommodate more guests. I positioned our new white tapestry sofa to the side of the freshly cut Christmas tree.

That year our family went to a church member's farm and cut an old-fashioned cedar tree. It was perfect for gathering around the Christmas tree, as it stood tall and the cedar fragrance filled the room. It added a special touch to this Senior Adult Christmas party.

I laid coasters out for people to set their punch cups. The trash can was empty and ready for throwaway items.

An hour into the party Bob comes to me.

"Someone has spilled red punch on the front of the sofa."

"Oh, the sofa is scotch guarded, no worries."

Then I saw the stain. Oh, my! Not a slight stain, but a large one. A sweet lady dropped her entire cup of red punch and a wide red stain covered half the front of the sofa cushion.

Okay, now I'm supposed to stay in control and forgive, right? I wasn't sure I could!

Had someone been clumsy and careless? Do I ever have red punch for children in my living room? As I dabbed at the stain, I thought, no way!

And then it hit me, what's more important—the sofa or the sweet elderly lady?

Humiliated and so apologetic she kept saying, "Will it be okay?" "Will it be okay?"

The actual question was, 'will I be okay?' I needed to be gracious and stay calm. And get a grip. It's just a sofa, a white tapestry sofa.

The Devil hammered at me. After all, I worked hard for that sofa.

I dabbed at the stain. He whispered in my ear, you wrote six months of Bible study lessons for middle-school-aged kids. The money you earned bought that sofa.

I've got to get a grip. People are watching me. I sensed them thinking, what's Judy going to do? My actions would speak louder than words. With God's help, I remained calm and forgave the lady who made the mess.

That stain was visible on our sofa for years. We tried count-less treatments to get the red out. One Christmas, someone gave me a handmade white crocheted blanket that I laid over the back of the sofa to hide the stain. The blanket helped me forget the time my emotions nearly overtook me.

When I removed it from the sofa, the stain was still visible. A reminder that material things do not bring happiness or con-tentment. Joyfully accepting Jesus as Lord and Savior will bring peace and contentment. And I remember, it's just a sofa.

Christmas Changes

'Twas the week before Christmas and all through the house, decorations were shining, but I was a grouch. Cards mailed and shopping completed. No thanks to Amazon or Shutterfly, they didn't exist. Gifts yet to deliver and mail. What to do? What to do?

I wasn't enjoying the Christmas season at all. And I'm the one who loves everything about Christmas. Could I pull the shades, crawl in bed, and forget about all the hoopla?

The family gifts needed wrapped, and peanut brittle pre-pared for neighbors and friends. I was not ready.

Swamped and grumpy. Why did we book every night with programs, parties, or dinners? Instead of fun evenings at home with our two little boys, they spent evenings with the babysitter.

Christmas is hard work. I tried my best to make the holiday fun. I wanted to be hospitality-sensitive, but it was difficult. The reason for the season? What was it? Oh yes, Jesus' birthday.

Christmas can be difficult. Sometimes dreaded. Our first year of marriage, we traveled two and a half hours to visit my parents on Christmas Eve. Then on Christmas Day, we drove ten hours to Pennsylvania to visit Bob's parents.

The next several years, to make it fair, we took turns where to spend Christmas day—mostly in the car. Thinking back, we were young and foolish, wanting to please everyone.

As we would drive home a couple days later, we were exhausted and wondering, how stupid can we be? Why are we doing this? Every year we spent Christmas on the interstate.

One year, Bob's wise Mother said, "You need to stay home for Christmas and start your own family traditions."

I thought, yes! And then my heart skipped a beat. But, but what about our extended families?

Bob's Mother was right. Those lengthy drives to Pennsylvania on icy, snow-covered roads resulted in some tense moments. Our family's safety was more important than taking a chance traveling year after year. It became the perfect time to start our own family traditions. And we did.

But nothing stays the same. As the years passed, both boys married and lived in town. We saw them often. But we wanted to be fair to our boys and their wives' families who also had traditions. So, we gave our sons the opportunity to decide when to have the Russell Family Christmas Celebration. Sometimes Christmas day, sometimes a few days prior or later.

Our family will often celebrate birthdays and holidays on off days too.

When Rusty and his family moved from Louisville to Florida, it was hard seeing them go. He accepted the lead pastor position at a church in South Florida. It thrilled us for their fresh beginning, yet we hated knowing this would be the end of our routine Russell celebrations.

We were visiting them and somewhat expected the sad announcement that they would not be home for Christmas. Those words were hard to swallow, like a knife piercing my heart. I thought, 'whatever will be, will be'. You must keep smiling, encouraging, and loving him.

Three months later Rusty calls me and said, "Mom, I've

decided we are coming home for Christmas after all, early in the month. I hope it's okay."

"Okay? Yes!"

Is it possible he was homesick?

We knew that first year after Rusty moved would be different and we celebrated our family Christmas on December 10.

The hustle and bustle of a regular December 25th day was in the air. Decorations were up, baking finished, cooking completed, candles lit, and gifts wrapped. The excited grandchildren never once complained.

We realized we had two weeks left before Christmas when we crawled into bed that night. We can enjoy parties, gatherings, and have Christmas again with our Louisville family. Although not as elaborate as the 10th with everyone. Should we do this every year? Once you have prepared, and the celebration has started, you don't even realize it's not December 25.

In today's culture, blended families make lots of concessions for holidays, particularly Christmas.

A divorce has divided the family, and you need to decide who buys that enormous gift for your child. To make Christmas easier for you and your family, check in with your ex. Decide on a budget and divide up the gifts.

Make Christmas plans early because several families are involved. Will it be celebrated at one or both parents or grandparents' home? Which day works best for each family? Regardless of the day, it's the spirit and love of a family coming together to celebrate Jesus' birthday that's important.

So, make a list and check it twice. Get a good night's sleep and don't wait until mid-December to prepare for Jesus' birthday.

I try to start early now and decorate less, pare down and rest so we all can enjoy Christmas. The dinners, parties, gift-buying, Christmas card mailing, and grocery store shopping will get finished, but maybe not as you pictured after browsing all those photos on Pinterest or Instagram.

But what is most important? The time or location or whether everyone we love is present? Or the number of presents received or how we have decorated our home? Do all those things decide if our Christmas celebration is special? Or remembered?

Remember whose birthday we are celebrating.

CHAPTER 17

Memorable Dinner Parties

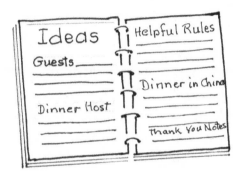

"A cheerful heart is good medicine, but a
crushed spirit dries up the bones."

Proverbs 17:22, NIV

DID YOU EVER wonder about the proper etiquette for arriving at
a dinner party? Do you send a handwritten thank you note or
email or text? Should you take a hostess gift?

What can you do to make your dinner party more successful?

We've hosted and attended dinner parties, large and small.
Many provided me with lessons and ideas I want to remember.

One stands out to me as strange, interesting, different, and
unforgettable.

An Absent Hostess

We arrived at the appointed time and the host met us at the door, greeting us with hugs. I kept wondering, where is his wife? The dining room table was ready. I could help if needed. Last-minute preparations can be overwhelming. Still no wife.

Everyone waited in the family room nibbling crackers and cheese. 45 minutes after everyone arrived, she came into the room, looking refreshed, with no apology.

We asked what happened. And her answer? Taking a nap! A nap?

The evening was enjoyable and relaxed as we visited with friends. But the hostess napping while we were waiting in their family room was strange.

The idea to rest is good, but plan on doing it before guests arrive. A nap or sitting in the easy chair with your feet propped up for 20 minutes can give you the extra boost of energy needed for the evening.

Honored Guests

In contrast to that evening, we were the honored guests at the home of the president of a large university. The President and his sweet wife greeted us at the door of their lovely old southern home, overlooking a massive river. We shared hugs, and they introduced us to the other guests.

Students from the university were servers and offered guests hors d'oeuvres in the parlor.

They invited everyone into the dining room. The President's wife stood at one end of the table and asked Bob to stand on her right. The President motioned me to stand at his right, at the opposite end of the table. Lovely place cards were arranged showing guests' names and where they were to sit. Everyone stood until the President's wife sat down in her chair. The rest of us were seated and enjoyed a lovely dinner and good fellowship.

That evening was one of observing great etiquette being put into action. The welcome at the front door, the introduction of guests, serving hors d'oeuvres, and seating at the table. It says to guests, "You are special."

Dinner in China

A missionary invited a group of evangelical ministers and their wives to Beijing, China, for meetings with Chinese government officials. The purpose of our trip was to extend the hand of Christian fellowship to Chinese leaders.

The American delegation prayed the Chinese leaders would understand that some of their best citizens were Christians.

It was the first time to meet the Chinese officials. We took gifts and presented them to the hosts.

When giving a gift to someone in China, you present it by extending both hands. This gesture shows respect to the one receiving the gift. When they give a gift, the receiver is to accept it with both hands.

The American Ambassador to China lived in Beijing and invited our delegation to his home. A staff member greeted us at the door. Imagine walking up to a total stranger's house in a foreign country and being greeted with, "Hello, Mr. and Mrs. Russell." It stunned us at first, as he didn't say anyone else's name. He introduced himself and talked about growing up in Louisville and going to Southeast Christian Church. What an honor to meet the young man and our hosts.

As we walked into their lovely home, we were immediately greeted and served tasty hors d'oeuvres. Everyone mingled together in a long narrow room, filled with chairs, sofas, and a grand piano in the corner. A very inviting place.

A seating chart was placed on a black velvet cloth laying on top of the grand piano. The chart showed the table number and listed our names. Impressed with this chart, I made a mental note for the future, as locating our table and place card was quick and easy.

We enjoyed a delicious dinner. But I shall never forget that seating chart. I've used the same idea several times when hosting a large dinner or luncheon seating people at tables in our home. Guests relax when they see where they are to be seated. And knowing who is at their table.

Ladies Luncheon

I hosted a sizeable group of ladies for a luncheon in honor of a young lady going to the mission field in Africa. The day before, friends came to set the tables and help me.

We worked on the seating chart, pairing ladies together, as we wanted them to enjoy one another's company. That's not a simple task.

We divided the chart up into dining room, breakfast room, porch, great room, and kitchen. There were 34 ladies coming, and I wanted everyone to have a seat. I placed the seating chart on a small easel and set it on the top of our grand piano in the great room. It was easy for guests to find their table, seat, and who would be sitting with them.

Rules for the Host, Hostess and Guest

Our culture today has changed so much over the years. The infamous Emily Post rules have changed and been updated. I did some research and discovered new insights for dinner party etiquette.

Host and Hostess

1. Plan your day for some rest before the party or dinner.
2. Select your date and the number of guests. If you seldom entertain, begin with a small group. Consider inviting people you know.
3. Serve a tried-and-true recipe. Nothing new. Or consider a catered menu. If catering the meal, it would be wise to do a taste test to make sure it is what you want to serve your guests.
4. Have everything ready at the announced time. Clean house, food ready, and the table set.
5. Park your car in the garage or elsewhere. Leave space for guests' cars.
6. Ask someone to help you.
7. Be prepared to change the topic of conversation if it gets out of hand.
8. If you have rules such as 'no smoking' in your house, tell your guests. Since no ashtrays are available, they should realize a 'no smoking' rule exists.
9. Guests should get the picture when it's time to go if you begin talking about the great evening you have had together. Remind people to check for any belongings they brought with them.

Guests

1. Answer the RSVP as soon as possible.
2. Do not arrive before the invited time. Wait in the car or drive around the block, if you are early. Note the starting time before you leave home. It is polite to be a few minutes late, but less than fifteen.

3. When running late, let the hosts know your ETA. Or suggest that they start without you.

4. If you want to bring an unexpected guest, clear it with the hostess ahead of time.

5. Leave your phone in your purse or coat pocket. Don't bring it to the table.

6. Taking a hostess gift is a pleasant gesture. Flowers in a vase are best, as the hostess may not have one available. Or have an arrangement delivered earlier that day.

7. When the hostess asks about your dietary restrictions, offer to bring a dish for the dinner. If she doesn't ask, say nothing. Just eat what you can.

8. If you see the hostess needs some help, be willing to jump in and help her. Offer to help remove the dishes from the table after the meal. Maybe load the dishwasher?

9. If you only know the host and hostess, come prepared to ask engaging questions of the guests you just met. But don't monopolize the conversation.

10. Send a handwritten thank you note to your host and hostess the next day. Everyone likes to receive a thank you for their efforts. Just a few words such as, "Wow, thank you. We enjoyed the evening and dinner." In today's culture, some say an email is okay. But to me, handwritten notes are more meaningful than high-tech alternatives. When you write a card of thanks, buy the stamp, and take the time to mail the card, it communicates, "we were blessed to be in your company". Facebook and Instagram are not the places to say thank you. Those not invited may get their feelings hurt.

CHAPTER 18

A Dress-up Party

"I, even I, am he who blots out your transgressions, for
my own sake, and remembers your sins no more."

Isaiah 43:25, NIV

THERE ISN'T A girl alive that doesn't enjoy getting dressed up for
special occasions. When the invitation arrives, what are your
first thoughts?

Yay! And then, oh dear, what will I wear?

It's not always easy to have the perfect dress hanging in
your closet for an event. Satan puts discouraging thoughts in
our minds. You need a stylish brand-new dress, you've worn

that one too many times. Not in style now, doesn't fit anymore, and it's ugly.

I think a sixth sense in girls stirs us to manage something, like buying a stylish new dress, or borrowing or renting one if needed. It is fun to get dressed in a fancy outfit for a special event.

I announced at our pastors' wives' monthly meeting an idea of a semi-formal party for Valentine's Day with our husbands. It thrilled the ladies, as Valentine's Day was in four weeks. A high tea will be perfect for our pastors to show appreciation for their wives. And ladies love tea parties.

My friends who catered tea parties worked with me to decide what tasty and hearty sandwiches, scones, clotted cream, jams, and assorted desserts were the best choices. And for sure, a variety of flavorful bottomless cups of hot tea.

I found pink and white striped chintz fabric on sale that was heavy enough to drape for tablecloths. I cut the fabric to fit each table and, thankfully, there was no need to sew hems. Besides, I'm a terrible seamstress!

We borrowed tables and chairs from the church and placed them throughout the house. But we needed several bouquets of flowers for centerpieces, and my budget didn't allow for elaborate arrangements.

Idea! Why not call the funeral home near us? What prompted me with that idea, I do not know.

I was eager, yet nervous, for their answer as I punched in the number.

"Hello, sir. I wondered what you do with leftover floral arrangements from funeral services?" Explaining my idea and why I wanted the flowers.

"Yes ma'am, we always have several arrangements we give away or throw away."

"Oh my, you throw them away?"

"Yes, we have several services this week and can save arrangements for you."

Later that week, I stopped by the funeral home to pick up the arrangements. Oh, my goodness! There were enormous baskets of roses, mums, carnations, lilies, tulips, and greenery, enough for making smaller arrangements for the tables.

My friend came and helped me as ladies love to help with interesting and fun needs. If someone is more talented than me in a particular field, I'm not afraid to ask for help.

The Concert Master of the Louisville Orchestra, a friend and a member of the church, arranged for a stringed quartet to play music that evening.

It will be an evening of stringed music, semi-formal dress, flowers, and high tea. The invitation read, 7:00 p.m. in the evening at the Russell's.

I was excited for this special evening honoring our pastors' wives. A perfect occasion for ladies to dress up and their husbands to wear suits and ties.

Everything was ready for the tea and I was excited. Guests will sit at tables throughout the house, including the four bedrooms upstairs.

The caterers wore white blouses, black skirts, black bow ties, and white aprons. Perfect. Place cards were at each place setting.

Our meal will take longer as there were several courses and lots of hot tea to drink.

There were 25 couples coming. Yes, 25. It will fill our house. The guests arrived.

As one couple came in, my heart sank. The wife wore a lovely party dress. But her husband? Well, he came in wearing a tee shirt and jeans. What happened? Didn't he see the invitation? I guess he didn't get the memo?

I couldn't say a word. Although everything in me wanted to scream and send him home to change. Might a lesson in respect be proper? Respect for the host and hostess? But more so, respect for his wife?

What happened? I was sickened. He stood out. I swallowed hard and smiled and tried to be as cheerful and kind to him as to everyone else.

To this day, years later, I wonder, 'Should I have said something? Made fun?' No. Only kind words were the right response. Someday, will he remember? Did his wife fuss at him when they got home?

The night was a success. The guys even enjoyed the high-tea dinner. And their wives looked stunning and happy.

To close out the evening, each lady would receive a love letter and a long-stemmed red rose from her husband.

Tears flowed as the wives opened their envelopes and read words of love and appreciation from their husbands. Hugs and kisses brought laughter. The perfect ending to a special night.

The house became quiet, and we began putting things back in place. In one bedroom, I flipped on the fan. Something was spinning through the air. I discovered it was one of our guest's place cards.

While continuing to clean and straighten things, I found more hidden place cards. They were on a lampshade, tucked behind a picture, and under furniture.

As I was getting ready for bed, I found one of our pastor's place cards in my lingerie drawer! Laughing, I thought, where else will we find place cards? Are there more? I didn't see any.

The next day, I found place cards hidden downstairs behind picture frames, tucked between books, under the corner of a chair. They were in all kinds of places. It was like searching for a pot of gold as I began looking everywhere and wondering if there were more. I guess everyone got that memo.

What do I remember about that evening? Not the guy in jeans and tee-shirt, the delicious food, the flowers, the fancy table settings, or the stringed music. But it was the fellowship, pranks, and laughter we remember more. I am thankful that our pastors and their wives felt comfortable enough to hide their place cards somewhere interesting.

Those kinds of evenings make entertaining fun and memorable and worth all the effort one puts into planning and working.

What is High Tea?

Have you ever thought about what *High Tea* means and about having it for an evening meal? Full Tea is an afternoon tea or Low Tea served here in America. Often, we hear that tea called High Tea.

In Britain, afternoon tea is for the wealthy and served midafternoon between 3:00 p.m. and 5:00 p.m. Since they do not have dinner until 8:00 p.m., the British need something in between lunch and dinner. Thus, they will have small sandwiches with light fillings and small sweets.

What the British call Afternoon Tea, we in America have in a tearoom for lunch. Sandwiches without a crust, scones, and other small light desserts are prepared and served. Ladies love going to a tearoom for lunch.

In resort areas, a hotel will serve Afternoon Tea after 3:00 p.m. and call it High Tea. It sounds fancier than Afternoon Tea.

The tradition for a British High Tea was for the working people. Similar to our American evening meal, which we call supper or dinner. They serve high tea after 6:00 p.m. when people get home from work. This can be meat pies, heavier meat-hearty sandwiches, along with savory sweets and scones.

Today, we may invite friends for heavy hors d'oeuvres instead of a sit-down dinner. This gathering resembles a high tea.

Ask the ladies to bring their favorite teacup to a party and tell their story behind the treasured cup.

Let's meet for tea sometime, okay?

CHAPTER 19

Caring Well for Our Guests

"When a foreigner resides among you in your land, do not mistreat them. The foreigner residing among you must be treated as your native-born. Love them as yourself."

Leviticus 19:33, 34, NIV

WHAT A TREAT it is to be away from home as an overnight guest to rejuvenate and enjoy time away. It is just as enjoyable to provide that experience to guests in our own homes. We all like being pampered. Pampering our house guests is a blessed form of hospitality too.

An Incredibly Hospitable Experience

Sheep grazed in the green fields while chestnut-colored horses ran along the white rail fence. The view was spectacular as we drove up a narrow tree-lined road. The manicured lawn with trees, shrubs, and plants surrounded the main house and cottages.

We arrived at our specified time, and two gentlemen were waiting to greet us.

"Welcome to Blackberry Farm, Mr. and Mrs. Russell. We welcome you and are here to help you during your stay with us." Each one reached out to extend a hand in greeting.

Both grabbed our luggage and placed them on a golf cart. One gentleman parked our car while the other drove us to our cottage. Our driver was excited to share the story of Blackberry Farm.

Spellbound with this tranquil setting, my heart thumped with excitement. The birds were singing and breezes rustling through the trees. Everything was beyond belief.

I stepped onto the porch of our cottage and peered through the open door. Inside our cottage room was an exquisite and romantic couple's retreat.

The canopy bed appeared to whisper, come climb in under the white down comforter and plump pillows. A fire was burning in the fireplace. Its warmth beckoned us to come sit awhile. Soft music was playing and there were snacks and bottles of water on the coffee table that sat in front of a yellow upholstered sofa.

Lights throughout the room were lit, adding to the ambiance. 'Am I in Heaven?' I didn't want to leave.

Our driver carried our luggage inside, placed them on luggage racks, and hung up our garment bags. He showed us how to work the TV remote, thermostat, and fireplace controls.

"I will pick you and Mr. Russell up at 5:35 p.m. as your dinner seating is at 5:45 p.m. Do you have questions?"

"No, thank you. You've been very helpful."

That was our introduction to Blackberry Farm in the Tennessee foothills of the Great Smoky Mountains. Friends gifted us with three nights. I was about to pop; I was so excited.

At 5:35 p.m., our driver took us to the main house for dinner. We waited in the sitting room. The host greeted us.

"Good evening, Mr. and Mrs. Russell. Follow me, please. Your table is here. Will this be okay?"

A white starched tablecloth covered the table that sat in front of an enormous window overlooking the foothills of the Smoky Mountains and Blackberry Farm.

Candles on the table were glowing in the dimmed light. Fine china, silverware, and folded napkins laid just so on the table. An artistic floral centerpiece complimented the tablescape.

"This is perfect. Thank you, sir."

As we looked out the window, the scenery left us calm and peaceful. Experiencing this staff's unbelievable kindness was beyond my comprehension. Everything we ate came from the gardens and fields at Blackberry Farm. The salad plates were icy cold to the touch and the lettuces and greens crisp and tasteful. It was near perfect.

I don't care for green peppers, even if fresh from the garden. So, I pushed them to the side of my plate. When our server came to pick up our salad plates, he said, "I will make a note that you don't care for green peppers, Mrs. Russell."

"It's okay. No problem. I'm just not a big fan of peppers." We continued eating our delicious dinner and enjoying the peaceful evening.

I forgot about the peppers when I ordered a quiche the next morning. Our new server said, "I understand you dislike green peppers, Mrs. Russell. I will tell the chef to drop them from your quiche". Last night's server made a note about the green peppers. I thought, what incredible hospitality. No wonder it's so special here.

Several years later, we wanted to celebrate our fortieth wedding anniversary by doing something special. Just the two of us. So, we returned to Blackberry Farm for a few days.

The landscaped grounds were bursting with gorgeous flowers and manicured shrubs and trees. Our pretty cottage and meals were again exceptional. Notes about my dislike of green peppers were still in their book. Can you imagine that?

Fifteen years later we went back to celebrate our 55th wedding anniversary. It was near the end of the lockdown and Covid-19 quarantine. I wondered if their hospitality and care for guests were the same.

When driving down the country road and getting closer and closer to the Farm, one feels the heavy loads of daily pressures being lifted. Ah.

As we pulled up the driveway to check in, the farm staff was waiting to greet us. It was as if we were family, coming for a visit. No hugs, just happy greetings.

Even though they wore black masks to protect their guests and themselves, each one showed kindness, was helpful, and smiled with their eyes. They wanted our stay to be the best. And it was! Their attention to detail was amazing.

They took us to our suite. The view of the Smoky Mountains was breathtaking.

At breakfast on our last day, we ordered a box lunch to take with us on our drive home. The Maître d' said, "I see you have no allergies to food, but you don't like green and red peppers." They still had data that I didn't like peppers!

The Blackberry Farm staff is determined to make your stay the very best. Their incredible example of great customer service is like no other I've experienced.

My times there have convicted me to be more intentional when guests come to our home, whether overnight or for a couple of hours.

Although most of our homes can't match the amenities of Blackberry Farm, we can all add a few improvements.

Preparing for Overnight Guests

"One day Elisha went on to Shunem, where a wealthy woman lived, who urged him to eat some food. So, whenever he passed that way, he would turn in there to eat food. And she said to her husband, "Behold now, I know that this is a holy man of God who is continually passing our way. Let us make a small room on the roof with walls and put there for him a bed, a table, a chair, and a lamp, so that whenever he comes to us, he can go in there." One day he came there, and he turned into the chamber and rested there." (2 Kings 4:8-11, ESV)

A book I read several years ago featured an Elisha Room. The author wrote about a special room in your home for guests to rest and relax while visiting. So, I made an Elisha Room.

Our oldest son Rusty was living out of town, and the extra bedroom in our home made a perfect Elisha Room.

I thought, how can I make it special for ladies and men? Please know that change didn't happen overnight. It's still a work in progress. I've taken years to get our guest room ready, and I'm still gathering items. For example, we need an iron and ironing board close by for guests.

Oh, so you don't have a separate room for guests? The one we had in our first home doubled as Bob's office when we were first married. I had to improvise and do my best to make guests comfortable. If you have clean sheets, extra pillows, and plenty of blankets, you can host overnight guests. They will love you for opening up your home.

Several times, I fixed a bed on one of our sofas for guests. Consider this—if you are making guests' beds in a busy room, you might set up a folding screen or stretch up some curtains or sheets to block off an area for their privacy.

You might need to use a child's room for your guests. Make sure your children are sleeping elsewhere in your house, though. Children love to bunk together in one of their rooms and sleep on the floor. Kids can make memories spending a few nights together "camping out" with cousins and friends.

Sofas, twin air mattresses, or blanket pallets on the floor will work great for the younger guest and your children. Kids and sleeping bags are an easy fix.

Sometimes, all seven of our grandkids came to spend the night at Nana and Pop's. Each grandchild had their own sleeping bag and pillow. We made pallets on the family room floor. Not much sleep, but lots of fun on those nights. As they grew older, we graduated to large air mattresses.

I hope you will plan on having overnight guests often. Begin the day with a prayer, asking God to bless your preparations and your guests. When the doorbell rings, you are ready to greet your guests with a handshake or a hug.

Show guests their room and help carry luggage. Ask them if they need a glass of water, soft drink, or a cup of coffee. Invite them to be seated in the family room or kitchen. If we, as hostesses, will stay relaxed and at ease, our guests will too.

When having overnight guests, remember, your guest room will not be Pinterest or Blackberry Farm perfect. Mine isn't! But we can make it look special. The bed is the most important piece of furniture in your guest's room. Your room should exude a welcome and one that will coax your guest to curl up and rest.

Need a starting point? Buy nice sheets, good pillows, and plenty of blankets and make the bed. Add a small bouquet of fresh flowers. Do something simple as some folks may be allergic to flowers.

Place a tray of snacks, including a couple new magazines on a table. Roll up the magazines and include a note saying welcome and please keep the magazines. Add a Bible and some books on a table with a good lamp. There you have it. An impressive start!

Will your guest be sharing a bathroom with others? How

about providing a drawer or shelf just for them? Remove the counter clutter and place a fresh bar of soap in a soap dish.

Tie a ribbon around a set of towels that includes a bath towel, hand towel, and washcloth. Prepare two or three sets of towels, one for each day they are visiting. Refresh the set if they stay longer, or need clean towels.

The ribbon-tied towels say, "welcome" as they lay at the end of the bed along with the magazines or a book.

Know their food allergies and other needs. We want our guests to relax and remember the time in our home, thinking, 'I hope they invite us back'.

I know you will have a magnificent guest bedroom ready for your next guest. You will be surprised with the items already in your home, waiting to be used.

Items for a Guest Room

1. A rack or low table along the wall or floor space for luggage.
2. Empty the closet, if possible, and add lots of hangers plus a laundry basket for dirty towels.
3. Empty a few drawers.
4. Frame instructions for accessing Wi-Fi.
5. A small electric coffee pot or teapot and cups. Place assorted coffees, sugar, packaged creamers, tea bags, snack bars, candy, and gum in a basket or on a tray. Give your guest a kitchen tour to find more items.
6. At least two sets of white washcloths, hand towels, and bath towels for each guest. Tie each bundle with a ribbon, or show guests where they are in the linen closet.
7. Place disposable three-ounce plastic-coated cups in a small container at the sink or on a folded paper towel or tissue.

8. Stock a small basket with new travel-sized toiletries, such as a new toothbrush in a packaged wrapper, toothpaste, shampoo and conditioner, bath gel, bath soap, body lotion, hairspray, hairbrush, comb, razor, shaving cream, and mouthwash.

9. Paper products: toilet paper rolls, tissue box (one in the bathroom and one in the bedroom), a paper towel roll, an assortment of feminine products stored under the sink in a basket or in the closet.

10. A basket for their personal toiletry items they can place on a shelf or in an empty drawer.

11. Hairdryer, curling iron, and hot rollers.

12. Trash can in the bedroom and one in the bathroom.

13. Information about the city where you live: Shops, churches, museums, and restaurants.

14. Place an extra throw or coverlet on the bed or chair for covering for a nap.

15. Comfy soft robe in the closet and a nightgown in an empty dresser drawer.

16. Small alarm clock in the guest room and a clock in the bathroom.

17. Small fan to help circulate the air if no ceiling fan.

18. Show them how to adjust the window shades if tricky.

19. Small flashlight or battery-powered candles with a remote control.

20. Night light in the bathroom.

21. Reading glasses.

22. Bible and devotional books. Include a couple recent books for them to read.

23. Small pitcher of ice water that includes a glass and napkins. Or water bottles.

24. Power strip and a charger for phones and computers.

25. Clean blankets in the closet and bed pillows (hard and soft) on the bed. Pillows need to be new. No stained limp pillows you took from another bed.
26. Towel bars in bathrooms.
27. Hooks for hanging robe and clothes in the bathroom.
28. Write on an index card the keypad code for your house security alarm, or make a house key available.
29. Mirror on the bedroom wall.
30. Hand mirror in a bathroom drawer.
31. Notepad, pens, envelopes, paper, a small table or desk with a chair and lamp.
32. Air freshener spray.
33. Instructions for remote controls for TVs or other remote-controlled devices: such as fireplaces, Alexa, lights on timers, and when the water sprinkler systems start.
34. Tylenol and Advil. Give guests a choice. They may have medical restrictions.
35. Earplugs in a cellophane bag. Throw away used ones.
36. Q tips
37. A comfortable chair or love seat and a small desk or table will add to your guests' comfort level.
38. TV or radio in the room or nearby.
39. A plunger for the toilet, stored in the closet.
40. White sheets—if makeup gets on a pillow or spills on the sheets, they will be easy to bleach when laundered. Wash and replace on the bed after guests leave. Then you are ready for your next guests.

Tips on guest bed linens. I always tuck the edges of the clean sheet in between the mattress and box springs. Then I know that the bed is ready for our next overnight guest. If it has been several weeks or months between guests, wash the sheets to freshen them. Or toss in the dryer with a fragrant sachet for a few minutes. Or you can spray the sheets with a nice quality linen spray that is scented or unscented. Le Blanc linen care products are one of my favorites.

I realize this list is long. Before you throw this book at me, know these are just suggestions. Lots of these items you will find in your house. I have gathered items for our guest bath and bedroom over several years. I find ideas when I travel and read articles and blogs. Plus, we don't have a TV in our guest rooms. We don't have an accessible iron or ironing board either. That's more the ideal. Maybe I'll even have those sometime. Enjoy planning and fixing up your guest room.

Here is an idea--consider a night for you and your husband to sleep in your own guest room sometime. Just for fun. It might surprise you how much you enjoy your own personal get-a-way.

CHAPTER 20

Brotherly Love: Phil and Andy

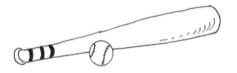

"This is my commandment: Love each other in the
same way I have loved you. There is no greater love
than to lay down one's life for one's friends."

John 15:12, 13, NLT

INSEPARABLE, THOSE TWO. When you saw one boy, you saw the
other. They were two little guys in the church nursery together, enjoyed overnighters in each other's homes, hung out
at school. They played on the same basketball and baseball
teams. We assumed their friendship would last forever. Every
year they watched their dads play in the National Christian
Church Softball Tournament and each boy took their turn being
batboys.

I remember one time when our family played the game
Pictionary and Andy played with us. Phil's word was "alfalfa".
I might have drawn a field of grass, but Phil began sketching a
picture of a boy whose hair stood up at the crown. Three seconds into drawing, Andy yells out, "alfalfa!" Phil's picture was

of the boy in the Little Rascals movie named Alfalfa, and his drawing was a close resemblance. Those boys read each other's minds.

When Phil was fourteen, he learned Andy was moving to another state. We were heartbroken and Phil was devastated.

Determined to do something special for his friend, he began searching through photographs of the two boys. Dozens of photos of them as infants, toddlers, preschoolers, grade-schoolers, and middle-schoolers lay scattered all over the top of our stereo. He made slides of the photos as he worked to mask the grief for his friend.

He sat in front of our stereo for hours, working and listening to the great song Michael W. Smith and his wife wrote titled "Friends." The lyrics rang so true for the boys' friendship. "Friends are friends forever if the Lord's the Lord of them."[23]

I peeked around the corner as he worked and wept for the boys. Thinking about it now, I am brought to tears. Not only was Phil losing his best friend, but our entire family would lose close friends.

We loved Andy's family. They loved us.

His mother and dad were part of a new church plant, Southeast Christian Church. Their elders asked Bob to be the pastor. We said yes and moved to Louisville. Andy's family was part of that ministry. They accepted us as one would old friends and family. We spent many hours in each other's homes.

Both families enjoyed watching basketball games on TV, attending sporting events, eating ice cream after church on Sunday nights, spending Christmas Eve together, and celebrating our kids' birthdays.

We showed them acts of hospitality and love like we would to a member of our family. Yes, we were family, and we were all part of the family of God.

We spent many Sunday nights in hilarious laughter and great discussions sitting at our tables eating pizza or hotdogs.

Time spent together talking and dreaming about the future of our church. We would miss those evenings when they moved.

Phil spent tedious hours on his project, and then it was time for the premier showing. Bob and I, along with Phil's older brother Rusty, gathered in the living room and waited to view the slide show. My heart pounded.

The music played. "Though it's hard to let you go ... a lifetime's not too long to live as friends."[24] Photos dissolved and faded in and out. The song *was* the perfect choice in this mini-production.

Andy's family wanted to see the show. We gathered to view the moving testimony of the boy's 14 years of friendship. Tears dropped onto our cheeks. "Though it's hard to let you go, in the Father's hands we know, that a lifetime's not too long to live as friends."[25] What a unique way of saying thank you for a long friendship. The years of blessings, love, and gracious hospitality are long remembered.

Andy came back to go to high school in the city he called home. He missed his grandparents and his best buddy, Phil. A few years later Andy's family moved back. But during their years away, Andy often stayed in our home. We loved him as a son.

CHAPTER 21

Reverse Hospitality: The Laying of the Rugs

"When Jesus reached the spot, he looked up and
said to him, 'Zacchaeus, come down immediately.
I must stay at your house today.'"

Luke 19:5, NIV

TALK ABOUT A major tossing of stuff! We lived over 28 years in
our Parkshire Court house and we needed to toss out, give away,
take to the consignment store, and if uncertain, pack things to
sort through later. There were a gazillion boxes filled, stacked,
and waiting to arrive and get unpacked in our new home.

Moving day arrived. Both of us were excited and sad. We
knew looming ahead was the unpacking of boxes, along with

getting everything put in place. We needed to get things in order within two weeks.

Two weeks later, the three 9 by 12 foot rugs and three pads I ordered arrived earlier than expected. Receiving a package early can excite me, but big rugs being delivered on Wednesday afternoon, three hours before eight preachers were to arrive for dinner, was too much.

It was the week of the Bob Russell Mentoring Retreat. We always hosted the eight ministers attending the retreat for dinner on Wednesday night in our home. Even though we stored boxes in the corners of rooms, it will not hinder eating and having conversations around our table. But where to leave rolled-up rugs and pads?

I said to the deliverymen, "I'm in a dilemma. We have eight people coming tonight for dinner. There is no time to lay rugs. Any suggestions?"

"We can leave the rugs right here ma'am, along the stair rail."

Can you imagine placing three 9 by 12 foot rolled-up rugs and pads just inside your front entry hall?

"Ok, go for it." I said, chuckling, "It will look as if I'm about to open a carpet store."

The preachers walked in that evening, and one asked, "Could we help unpack or move things?" Bob must have warned them we had just moved.

I about threw my arms around him in gratitude. "Could you?", I said.

Others chimed in, "Yes, we can help."

Laughing, I said, "Are you sure?" Hmm, maybe lay the rugs?

People want to feel useful and help. Let them.

When someone asks, "Can I help?" I will try to give them something to do. It makes my task easier and guests want to help because they appreciate the invitation and time you've given.

Have you ever thought about Jesus practicing reverse hospitality?

In Luke 19:1-6 NIV is the story of Zacchaeus.

"Jesus entered Jericho and was passing through. A man was there by the name of Zacchaeus; he was a chief tax collector and was wealthy. He wanted to see who Jesus was, but because he was short, he could not see over the crowd. So he ran ahead and climbed a sycamore-fig tree to see him, since Jesus was coming that way. When Jesus reached the spot, he looked up and said to him, "Zacchaeus, come down immediately. I must stay at your house today." So he came down at once and welcomed him gladly."

Zacchaeus wanted to see Jesus, so he climbed a tree. That action touched Jesus, and he invited himself to Zacchaeus's home.

It touched me with the offer of the retreat attendees to help.

"Could you lay the rugs after dinner?"

"Sure, we can. You tell us where and we can do it."

I was thinking, 'Oh my. What an incredible gift that will be!'

Earlier, when the delivery men left, I remembered our last month's retreat and how the guys offered to move boxes. Those eight preachers carried every packed box from the upstairs bedrooms and the downstairs lower-level family room to the music room on the first floor. It thrilled us. We knew the movers would be ecstatic.

Dinner was over, and the guys were ready to lay the rugs. They bounced up from their chairs and moved the furniture out of the way.

One by one they unrolled the rugs. I held my breath, thinking, let those rugs be the right size and color.

OOPS! I miscalculated the dining room rug placement by two inches. The corner of the rug needed to go under the china cabinet. They carefully removed the dishes from the cabinet, tilted it back, and slipped the rug under the edge.

A couple guys took the lead. As I stood there watching, they measured and smoothed out the edges of the rug. They stopped, stood, and eyed their work, to make sure everything was A-Okay. Well done. Within 20 minutes, they finished their work. They laid the three rug pads and three rugs. They placed the crystal dishes back in the china cabinet and positioned furniture back on the rugs.

Sixteen preachers gave their time and energy to help us. I didn't ask them; they offered. Has someone honored you with reverse hospitality?

I have two friends who are exceptional examples of jumping in to help. They gather dishes from the table and work until they are clean and dried. It is a wonderful gift of reverse hospitality.

My friend, who was born and raised in Russia, told me when someone has a birthday, they host a party or dinner. Yes, the honoree bakes the cake, cooks the food, cleans the house and everything is ready when guests arrive.

Reverse hospitality? Guests come to your home and you are the hostess and birthday honoree. Unusual twist, don't you think? I wonder if the wife and mother does this for everyone in her home?

In Western culture, hospitality is something we do to bless and honor people we've invited to our home. We prepare the meal and often say "no, thank you" when a guest offers to help.

But why not try some reverse hospitality? I'm not sure I would invite myself to have dinner at someone's home. But if you are a guest, offer to help clear the table, rinse off the dishes, wipe off counters, and sweep the floor. Or lay the rugs? That is a blessing to the hostess.

Bob has run into preachers at conventions and they say, "I was there the night we laid the rugs at your house."

They were excited to have dinner with us, be in our home, and help. Memories of doing good deeds will leave lasting impressions for the guests and you.

CHAPTER 22

Being a Good Houseguest

"When you enter a house, first say, 'Peace to this house.' … Stay there, eating and drinking whatever they give you, for the worker deserves his wages. Do not move around from house to house."

Luke 10:5,7, NIV

WHEN GOOD FRIENDS leave to go home after visiting a few days, I'm melancholy. Are you? I love the laughter, fun, and memories. Then guests leave, and there is an unnerving quietness. I miss the interaction, even if I am pooped.

Good friends left for home. The guest room bed linens needed to be laundered, and I noticed the nightstand drawer was still open. Inside was a set of car keys. I called our friends. The keys belonged to their other car.

"Yes, I can overnight the keys to you in the morning." They wanted to pay me for the cost. I said, "Thank you, but our guests are special and it will be my pleasure to return them to you."

Years earlier, we attended a convention in Dallas, Texas. After returning home, I noticed the message light on our house phone. It was from the housekeeping staff at the hotel where we stayed.

"Mrs. Russell, we found a drawer full of dirty clothes in your room after you checked out of our hotel. We think it's your husband's dirty laundry."

I called them back. Apologizing, "Yes, they are my husband's clothes. I am so sorry. How embarrassing! What can we do? I hate the inconvenience to your housekeeping people. Please thank them for us. Please let me pay for shipping costs and for the trouble we've caused your staff."

The gentleman answered with these gracious and kind words, "It will be our pleasure to return the clothes to him. Our guests are special and we don't treat them otherwise."

Isn't that a picture of gracious hospitality? I want to remember this gesture.

A few days later, we received a package from the hotel. I opened the box. Oh my, there was another box inside the first box. Someone wrapped the box of dirty clothes as if it was a gift.

I pulled back the white tissue paper, revealing Bob's clothes. No way. The hotel's housekeeping staff washed and dried his clothes, folded every piece and placed them in the tissue paper lined box! Can you imagine?

What an incredible gesture of hospitality. This was customer service beyond the call of duty. I want to go back.

I've left things and called our host or hotel and asked to have them returned. We've all left something important sometime, someplace. But this hotel's response was beyond gracious hospitality. Don't you want people to treat you like that?

As I remembered this story, I thought, 'how can I be a better houseguest?'

Dos and Don'ts for the Houseguest

1. Take a small hostess gift. If your host has children, include a coloring book and crayons or a book to read.
2. Unpack and hang clothes in the closet and place folded clothes in a dresser drawer, if provided.
3. Keep suitcase closed.
4. Make your bed each morning and keep your room tidy.
5. Pick up dirty towels and take them to the laundry room. Offer to launder them.
6. Keep the sink and counter in the bathroom cleared of your personal things.
7. Bring a two-gallon-sized plastic bag to hold all of your personal hygiene items. Store it out of sight if possible.
8. Know the morning and nighttime routine of your hosts and their family.
9. Make sure you give your host and hostess some space and alone time.
10. Depending on the length of stay, offer to buy a meal or two, or buy groceries.
11. Offer to set the table.
12. Help with cleaning up the kitchen.
13. When packing to return home; check the bathroom, under the bed, the drawers, and the closet for items you may have overlooked.
14. Ask about taking the sheets off of the bed. Put them in the laundry room and start the washer. Fold blankets and lay them on the foot of the bed with the pillows.
15. Straighten the room, turn off the lights, and open the curtains or blinds when you leave.
16. Mail a hand-written note to your hosts. Or leave one in the room.
17. Don't bring your pet. Leave them at home!
18. Appreciate your visit.

CHAPTER 23

Too Busy Not to Pray

"Rejoice always, pray continually, give thanks in all
circumstances; for this is God's will for you in Christ Jesus."

1 Thessalonians. 5:16-18, NIV

Rusty graduated from college on Saturday morning in Cincinnati, Ohio. Having multiple worship services at our church on Sunday morning added to the stress of a busy weekend.

We hosted a party with his friends at the college on Saturday after the graduation ceremony. Sunday evening, we would host a party at our house for Louisville friends. The next weekend was another party for our son Phil, graduating from high school. I could only think about parties and celebrations. Nothing else.

Sunday morning, I slept in and planned to go to the last service.

Five minutes before the first service began, Bob called, waking me from a dead sleep, saying, "Judy, did you forget the Sweet Spirit Singers are singing this morning?"

"Oh no." I sat straight up in bed. I had forgotten the Sweet Spirit Singers, a ladies' choir I directed, were singing at the morning church services.

"I'll hurry."

He said, "No, come the next hour."

Have you ever been so bogged down with activities surrounding a special event, such as a wedding or showers or graduations, you forgot something else important?

Linda, a wonderful lady and talented musician, helped me with rehearsals each week. But I hated laying this burden on her unannounced and unprepared.

Why didn't I check my calendar Saturday night? Spiritual responsibilities should be first. Getting up late, racing to church to meet the choir is not smart. I needed to put the evening party on hold for a few hours. What I needed was a spiritual lift now, not next week!

Yes, I was overwhelmed with preparing our boys' graduation parties. I needed to calm down and take a break. I needed time for worship.

Things were about me. My priorities were out of order. Pray later, read my Bible later, pray for the choir on the way to church. How selfish of me and how embarrassing! Maybe better words are "how stupid."

That experience taught me a lesson. When we get our hospitality priorities out of order, it is nearly impossible to recover. I was fortunate someone covered for me, and even though I volunteered, thankfully the music director didn't fire me.

To forget an event can happen. We sometimes think we are invincible, but we are not. I should have checked my schedule earlier. But I didn't. This was a good lesson to not schedule so many events close together. And I was so grateful for a morning of worship.

CHAPTER 24

Smart Phone and Hospitality

"Be kind and compassionate to one another, forgiving each other, just as in Christ God forgave you."

Ephesians 4:32, NIV

WHAT COMES TO your mind when you hear the word *hospitality*? Overnight guests? Kindness to those we meet? A smile while serving others?

Have you ever thought of your smartphone as a source of kindness and hospitality? A few chosen words can uplift and encourage. Use your mobile device to show kindness when connecting with friends and family, or even those you seldom see.

Do you know someone who suffers from an illness or has a family issue? It is easy to send multiple texts that land in seconds to smartphone contacts requesting urgent prayer. Or send a text to a friend suffering with cancer to share a word of kindness or just say "I love you and I'm praying for you." Add a scripture verse. That is digital kindness.

We feel lost without that little rectangular device in our hand or pocket.

It's handy when doing your Bible study lesson. You can search scripture apps and commentaries on particular subjects without having a pile of books on your desk.

Our two boys and their families lead busy lives and sending quick texts of encouragement, along with an *I love you*, is a thoughtful and hospitable gesture. And receiving quick texts back is a blessing. How thrilling to read, "I love you, Nana," from a grandchild in college, school, or out of state. A quick little love note from my husband when out-of-town makes me warm inside, and he doesn't seem so far away.

I enjoy connecting with friends, sending notes of encouragement and keeping up with them. A young actress reminded me of a friend's daughter. I sent her a short text, and she texted back within a couple of minutes, "I'm in Indonesia." Oh, my goodness! That's halfway around the world.

I'm thankful to connect with people through this unique digital device. Used correctly, the smartphone can show love, kindness, and hospitality to friends and family around the world.

Fun Ideas with A Smart Phone

Not only showing kindness with words, did you ever think of showing kindness by playing games with your friends?

Invite some couples for a digital game night at your house. The guests will use their smartphones. Our son and his wife gave us a game in which participants answer questions found on their phones. They may pull up photos they took, or do a search, etc. It's fun.

There are games you play with your family using your smartphone and the TV. It's called Jack Box TV. We played many times with our son and his family in Florida. It's a fun family game.

If you are hosting a party and a game involves using the guests' smart phones, suggest on the invitation that guests charge their phones before they come. Or have several phone cords available, just in case.

Smart Phone Kindness Tips

1. Do not assume the person receiving your text will recognize your phone number. Add your name to the text.
2. Keep your smartphone out of sight at meals and meetings. People are more important than texting. Don't answer texts unless it is an emergency.
3. Respond to texts within 24 hours.
4. Watch the auto-correct for mistaken words. It may not be a good correction of the word. I know. I've messed up.
5. When using a Bible app at church, silence the keyboard and lower the screen lighting.
6. Turn the phone off at weddings and funerals.
7. Don't assume everyone wants to see your family photos. Ask first.
8. Pray daily to be a good steward of time spent on your mobile devices. We all need boundaries and limits.

CHAPTER 25

An Atmosphere of Hospitality

```
┌─────────────────────────────┐
│ ┌─────────────────────────┐ │
│ │   Wednesday Night       │ │
│ │       Dinner            │ │
│ │      5:00 p.m.          │ │
│ └─────────────────────────┘ │
└─────────────────────────────┘
```

"He took the five loaves and two fish, lifted his face to heaven
in prayer, blessed, broke and gave the bread to the disciples.
The disciples then gave the food to the congregation."

Matthew 14:19, 20, MSG

As I DELVED into a bowl of old-fashioned yellow potato salad, I
thought about how much I looked forward to the Wednesday
night potluck dinners at our church.

Our church leadership thought it would be a grand plan in
getting families out to the midweek service. They were right. It
was a huge hit.

But church members bringing a potluck dish every week became
laborious. So, we began having dinners catered. People signed up
for the Wednesday night dinner on their roll call cards on Sunday.
They paid a small fee for their meal at the time of the dinner.

Since we were in a building program and would soon have a large, professional kitchen in our church, I volunteered to be in charge of our Wednesday night dinners. That means being the chef and cooking the dinners.

Yes, God was stretching me with this venture of cooking for several hundred people.

I was jumping out of my comfort zone. My only experience cooking for large groups was six weeks at church camp as the assistant cook.

I began reading and researching recipes and menus for big groups. Since it was pre-internet days, books became my primary resource. I talked with people who cooked for enormous groups at schools and church camps, asking lots of questions and watching them work. I still peruse magazines and the internet for fun and yummy food to serve people, whether a small or large group. Although now, most of our larger dinners hosted at our house are catered.

We zeroed in on six menus, rotating them each week. Several meals we cooked from scratch, and a couple were purchased already prepared. About every two months, we had "Clean Out the Freezer Night." It delighted cooks from shelters to come and pick up the leftover food.

Two wonderful ladies met me on Wednesday morning at 9:00 a.m. to begin the day.

One favorite meal for the weekly crowd was pork cutlets with a baked potato, side dish, and salad. Shirley, Georgia, and I browned the pork cutlets, layering them in large warming pans until full. Then we poured large cans of cream of mushroom soup over the meat. We placed the pans in the ovens at a low temperature and began simmering the meat all afternoon. By dinner time, the tender meat was perfect.

We parboiled baked potatoes. I guess you could say somewhat fake baked potatoes.

I discovered the method while our family was on vacation

in Colorado. We went to a rodeo show and dinner at a ranch. Cowboys, dressed in cowboy hats and rodeo gear, served us dinner. The meal was steaming hot and comprised of yummy meatloaf, spicy baked beans, cinnamon-flavored applesauce, a baked potato loaded with butter and sour cream, and a berry pie.

They told us how they cooked the baked potatoes. Scrub clean, wrap in foil, and boil in an enormous pot. It didn't take long for the pot to boil and cook the potatoes. You could even eat the skin if you desired.

Lots of recipes online say parboil and then wrap in foil and bake for 30 minutes. I say, "to each his own". I vote for wrapping in foil, parboiling, and that's it.

People loved that dinner hour. Still, people see me and say they wish they could have Judy's pork cutlets again. It's been over 30 years ago, and I can still imagine the smell of food cooking.

We served lasagna on Wednesday nights, too. The prepared meat sauce was layered between uncooked lasagna noodles in large warming pans and put in a low-temperature oven, cooking all afternoon.

Cubed steak was another favorite prepared by following the pork cutlet recipe. We served the steaks with a salad, hot rolls, butter, and a side dish along with baked or mashed potatoes.

Side dishes were often corn or green beans, seasoned like our grandmothers used to do. And lots of butter poured over mashed potatoes. We made the instant potatoes yummy with cream and butter. Our salad, packaged in enormous bags, was pre-washed and ready to serve.

A meal of spaghetti and tossed salad with slices of garlic bread was also a hit. The jars of meat sauce and cooked ground beef along with added Italian seasonings simmered all afternoon. We cooked the spaghetti, dropping it in boiling water. When cooked, we rinsed off the starchy residue in a colander with scorching tap water. The spaghetti poured into steam table pans, needed the starch residue rinsed off so it would not stick together. The chef doesn't want clumps of sticky spaghetti.

Those meals were fun and always included a dessert. A member of our church owned a bakery. On special occasions, we would order their sheet cakes. Or if we made sheet cakes ourselves, we bought icing from their bakery. Sometimes we served cookies or ordered pies from a factory in town. Kerns Kitchen Pies were the best, and they still bake their famous Derby pie.

It was the perfect opportunity to invite friends and family to the Wednesday night dinner and midweek worship services. Everyone enjoys a delightful meal and not having to cook or clean the kitchen.

The gymnasium in our church was perfect for a large dining space. But you know me. I felt we needed something to brighten the eating space. So, I bought several artificial floral arrangements for the eight-foot banquet tables. They looked real, and we stored them in cabinets, pulling them out for different seasons.

I found colorful plastic tablecloths to cover the tables, making everything more hospitable. Volunteers came each week to help set up the tables and chairs for dinner. Others put the tablecloths on the tables and arranged the floral centerpieces.

After dinner, people would gather the plastic tablecloths, wash them off, and if they were in excellent condition, fold them and store for the next week.

In those days we served dinner to over 300 people. It was fun, yet exhausting. But God was honored.

I've thought back about hospitality extended at those dinners. Hospitality shared as we greeted dinner guests who came through the buffet line. Hospitality given as people helped with last-minute preparations. There were hospitable men who lifted pots from the stove and poured ingredients into steam table pans. Others pulled hot pans out of the ovens and placed them on the steam table.

Then the clean-up jobs. Volunteers gathered silverware, pitchers, pots, and pans and ran them through the dishwasher. Others dried everything and put items back in the cabinets until the next time. Someone swept and mopped the floor, while others wiped off counters and cabinets. And some helped prepare leftovers for the freezer.

Once in a while, the food needed to cook longer and people patiently waited for a few minutes. Or, even worse, we ran out of food. A couple times I called KFC, hoping to get several large buckets of fried chicken. A substitute entree needs to be better than what guests expected.

As I pulled the keys from my purse and locked the kitchen door, I was thankful for another successful week.

Thank you, Lord, for the opportunity to host our Wednesday night people once again. It's been my pleasure to serve them in such a special way and give you the honor and glory.

CHAPTER 26

Radical Halloween

"Be devoted to one another in love. Honor one
another above yourselves. Never be lacking in zeal,
but keep your spiritual fervor, serving the Lord."

Romans 12:10, 11, NIV

"MOM, IS IT okay if a few players from Andy and Chapman's football team come over and go trick-or-treating with them in your neighborhood?"

Our neighborhood was great for trick-or-treating. The grandkids loved coming to our house on Halloween night. Since playing in a city football league and making lots of new friends, they wanted their buddies to join them and go trick-or-treating. They would meet at our house.

It seemed Halloween night came faster than usual that year. But we were ready. The pumpkins were lit and our favorite candy bars filled the trick-or-treat basket. Soon kids would knock on our door.

Our family started eating bowls of homemade hot turkey chili. The doorbell rang as we gulped down our first few bites. Wait, it wasn't 6:00 p.m. yet. I took a deep breath as I wiped my mouth and opened the front door. In bounced the first guest. He brought his mother too.

Moments later, lots of grade school boys rushed into our house, bringing their families. I didn't expect entire families to come, but how else could their children get here? Who would supervise their trick-or-treat time and take them home? I was thankful their parents came.

I'm not a big fan of people surprising me. Although, I love doing fun and surprising things for other people. These circumstances test me. Remember, I never wanted to marry a preacher. I didn't want to be in a situation when I needed to make quick decisions and be gracious and kind. But that night was different, and Halloween became an evening of unexpected hospitality.

Our two grandsons and their football friends began jumping up and down, eager to get going. Candy bars were as visions of sugarplums in their minds.

Parents dressed the children in their Halloween garb and everyone was ready. My camera was ready, too. Photos on Halloween night are a must at our house. The grandchildren enjoy skimming through old Halloween photo albums. They laugh at trick-or-treat outfits from years past and poke fun at each other.

The kids tolerated me and their parents as we coaxed them to stand still for a second or two. Finished with taking photos, we yelled, "GO!"

Those young trick-or-treaters leaped forward as if shot from a cannon, scrambling across the front lawn to our neighbors' houses.

Halloween night that year was one of the coldest I can remember. Rain pelted down and then it started spitting snow. It didn't stop the trick-or-treaters on a candy bar mission.

Some parents walked with their children, while others stayed at our house to care for the younger kids. Guests gathered in the kitchen, pulled up chairs and crowded around our kitchen table.

As I opened the cabinets full of toys in the family room, the younger children squealed with excitement. I hurried to grab my stash of orange plastic plates, napkins and cups for serving snacks.

Trick-or-treaters rang our doorbell every minute. I struggled to keep up with answering the door and serving our guests.

Bob tried his best to carry on a conversation. He asked, "Who is your favorite football team?" Our guests loved football and sports, and the conversation soon sprang into high gear. I have to admit it was an exciting evening, although exhausting and unexpected.

Chocolate chip cookies and hot apple cider along with salty snacks vanished before my eyes. One father, a former NFL lineman asked, "What else do you have to eat?"

Laughing as I rushed to answer the doorbell, I yelled back to him, "You can check the pantry. There is chili in the refrigerator. Help yourself."

And they did. Root beer, colas, and ginger ale lids started popping open. Snack bags pulled apart amid laughter and interesting stories from these new friends.

A little while later, squealing and giggling trick-or-treaters stormed into the house like a whirlwind. They kicked off their wet shoes and pulled off soggy costumes, throwing everything in a big wet heap.

As they dumped their load of sweet candy bars out on the floor, they started stuffing their mouths. Sticky candy juices began running down their chins. I grabbed napkins and encouraged them to wipe their faces and hands before chocolate dribbled all over their clean clothes and my beige carpet.

Oh my, was I glad I didn't have to put those kids to bed. They would be on a major sugar high half the night.

Toys and kids appeared to fly everywhere as they ran up and down the stairs to the basement, playing together. I sighed in relief, dropping on the sofa, thinking I'm too tired to move. Thankful though, that we said yes when our son asked to open our home for these friends.

Weary and whipped, I still enjoyed this gathering.

We saw these families while attending our grandson's football games and exchanged cordial greetings. Phil, our son, invited them to church. Put me to shame.

But that evening, they gathered around our kitchen table, laughing, asking questions, teasing, and telling their stories. To share our home with them was a blessing. And to think I almost said no.

Several times over the years, unexpected guests and students have stayed in our home. We've shared meals and provided beds, did laundry and packed lunches and snacks. There have been times I didn't think I could wash one more glass or clean up one more mess or remake one more bed. But I remember that those unexpected events are often the most enjoyable and memorable.

CHAPTER 27

Come to the Table

He took bread, gave thanks and broke it, ... saying, this is
my body given for you; do this in remembrance of me ...
After the supper he took the cup, saying, this cup is the new
covenant in my blood, which is poured out for you.

Luke 22:19, 20, NIV

AS A CHILD, every Sunday morning I watched my parents take
communion at church. They bowed their heads, held a piece
of bread and a cup of grape juice representing Jesus' body and
blood. I didn't understand how significant taking communion
was until I was older and accepted Jesus as my Lord and Savior
and was immersed for baptism. Since then, gathering around the
Lord's table has always held a special place in my heart.

Every year my mother volunteered to take a month and prepare the communion trays for the church's Sunday morning service. I remember wanting to help her.

The first time I prepared the emblems and washed each individual glass cup and polished the silver tray, I was nervous and wanted everything to be perfect.

My daddy carried the filled trays across the street to our church building. He gently placed them on a starched white tablecloth draped across the special table dedicated for communion emblems. Then he draped another starched cloth over everything to keep the flies off the trays. Our church building didn't have air conditioning, so, on Sunday mornings, they opened the windows to let the cool breeze come through—flies too.

Bob and I have taken communion in churches throughout our country and in foreign lands. We've taken communion in homes, hotel rooms, along the beach, and on vacation. One special place was while sitting on benches in the garden across from the tomb where Jesus had laid for three days.

A unique time taking communion was when I was with several thousand people at a conference. The morning speaker spoke about communion. He explained the meaning and how we should remember Christ's sacrifice. In his conclusion, his voice was soft, speaking with passion. I remember him saying, "Imagine you have a piece of bread and a cup of juice in your hands. Let's partake of communion together."

"Take the bread," he said. "Hold it on your tongue. Imagine the bread, as the body of Christ, ripped and torn apart for you and me. Leather strips with bits of metal fastened to the ends, cut into the flesh of Jesus and sliced open his blood vessels with every fierce blow. Thirty-nine blows. Blows to the body could kill a person being scourged."

I remember the conference speaker talking about the juice. "Imagine holding a cup of juice." He asked us to lift the cup to our lips and sip. He didn't want us to swallow just yet. He asked us to swirl the juice around in our mouth, remembering it represented the blood Jesus shed for us.

I couldn't help but think about Jesus' blood dripping on the ground around him and splattering against the soldier who delivered the fierce scourging blows. His thin skin pulled off as scourging blows grabbed shreds from his body. Skin covering ribs that protected his heart and lungs. I shudder, thinking of the cries of horrendous agony coming from his throat. Our Lord and Savior's precious body was being ripped open and bleeding for you and me.

I picture in my mind how a soldier shoved a crown of thorns onto Jesus' head. The sharp thorns pierced his brow, causing blood to flow into his eyes and drip off his beard. As we take communion, eat the bread and drink from the cup, we remember how Christ suffered and died for us.

I walked out of that conference session in silence. Thousands of us did. What an unforgettable and moving communion service. A time to remember that Christ loved us so much that he endured a brutal scourging and nailing to a rough wooden cross. He accepted the piercing in his side and death so that one day we will live with him in Heaven.

Today when I take communion, I often remember that morning's conference speaker and his message.

Sometimes, I picture in my mind, *The Passion of Christ* film, and the scourging of Jesus. The scene of skin, sweat, and blood flying in the air makes me appreciate God's incredible love even more.

I still get goosebumps as I remember the moment in that film when a huge tear dropped from Heaven as Jesus hung on the cross. This was God's gift of immeasurable love given to me a sinner. He wept and so did I.

That's ultimate hospitality.

Communion Around the World

They wanted us to be a part of their weekly Friday night family dinner. Lexington, Kentucky friends invited us, along with our friends to come for a special dinner. What fun that will be.

Their son and daughter and spouses lived in Lexington, too. The one couple just gave birth to a baby girl. I love spending time with young married couples. They are so energized, knowledgeable, and vulnerable. How heart-warming to see the love coming from the hearts of these couples.

"Where two or three are gathered in my name, there am I with them." (Matthew 18:20, NIV)

As we walked up the steps to our friends' townhouse, the whiffs of baked bread from the oven were in the air. Our hostess is my favorite bread baker. I was starving, or so I thought. My mouth watered for sure, as I knew what awaited us when we gathered around their table. I was not prepared for what happened next.

Our host asked if we minded taking communion together before we ate dinner. We were humbled when asked to be a part of their family's special time.

Matthew and Nancy's adult children and spouses and only grandchild were soon moving to Africa to work on the mission field. The work would be hard. Separation from a family they love would be difficult. The move would be stressful, as a foreign land and an unknown lifestyle awaited them. It is amazing how countless young couples give up so much, for so little, to share God's boundless love. It puts me to shame. These couples were ready to be soldiers in God's army. We continue to pray for them.

It honored us to have dinner with this family. We had mixed emotions as there will not be many more Friday nights to have communion together.

"Where two or three are gathered in my name, there am I with them." (Matthew 18:20, NIV)

As we each took our seat around the dining room table, I sensed a bonding. The gathering of believers in this intimate setting will be special.

I didn't know our host asked Bob to do a communion meditation.

He began.

> "I'm impressed with the symbolism in the Old Testament. There are many brief hints, mysterious types, that point to a coming Messiah and God's marvelous redemption. The more we study these prototypes, the more convinced we are that the Bible is the Word of God, and the more we all appreciate the depth of God's redemption in Christ. No human could ever come up with this.

> "A perfect example is the scapegoat in Leviticus chapter 16. Every year on the Day of Atonement, Yom Kippur, the holiest day of the year, a unique ceremony took place. The high priest stood before thousands of people with two perfect goats at his side. One goat is sacrificed for the sins of the people. The other goat set free.

> "The priest cast lots to decide which goat would be sacrificed. Then he slew the sacrificed goat, laid hands on the other goat, and confessed the sins of the people. That goat was taken outside the city and released.

"That's a fascinating symbol of the sacrifice of Jesus, hundreds of years before he went to the cross.

"Hebrews 10:4 NIV says, 'It is impossible for the blood of bulls and goats to take away sins.'

"Jesus was the sinless one, the perfect one. He was without spot or blemish, the Bible says in Isaiah 53:6 KJV, 'God laid on Him the iniquity of us all.'

"He died and we escape. We go free, even though we stand guilty of sin. Remember what took place before Jesus' sacrifice on the cross?

"John 18:39 tells us, 'It is your custom for me to release to you one prisoner at the time of the Passover. Do you want me to release *the king of the Jews*?' (NIV)

"Pilate, seeking a way to avoid condemning Jesus, yet appease the people, gave them a choice of two prisoners to release. 'Whom shall I release? Jesus, or Barabbas?'

"Barabbas was a known criminal, condemned to death as a murderer.

"Do you know what the name Barabbas means? Bar meant "Son of" (Simon Bar-Jonah). Bar–Abba. Abba means "Father." Barabbas was the son of the Father.

"The choice was between Jesus, who was the Son of God—the Son of the Father—and Barabbas, the son of the Father.

"The people chose Barabbas. Since he was in the cell nearby, he might have been able to hear the crowd, but not the questions of Pilate. I wonder if the sounds of 'crucify, crucify' then the chant, 'Barabbas! Barabbas!' were words that made him wonder about his outcome. When the guard came and called his name, he must have thought he was marching to his execution. Instead, Barabbas, who deserved execution, was led out into the streets of Jerusalem and released.

"1 Peter 3:18 NIV says, 'For Christ also suffered once for sins, the righteous for the unrighteous, to bring you to God'".

"As we take communion tonight as guilty sinners condemned to die, let's give thanks that Jesus set us free from condemnation and death as was Barabbas. Why? Because Jesus volunteered to be our sacrifice."

We sat spellbound. I thought, 'this moment is a picture of hospitality as we gather and take communion around a family table.' God sent his son to be our sacrifice. Jesus spent many hours around tables with people, teaching and communing together.

When we take communion every week with fellow believers, these two couples will take communion halfway around the world with believers.

I will never forget that unexpected time of hospitality and remembering Christ around their family table.

A Nurse's Compassionate Hospitality

It was the beginning of a beautiful Sunday morning. October 28, 2019. The date for the 116th Anniversary of South Louisville Christian Church. Bob preached that morning. Many folks who grew up going to South Louisville came back for this special service.

This church holds a special place in my heart. Their congregation started Southeast Christian Church along with several other Christian Churches over the past 50+ years. Tens of thousands of people now know Jesus because of the ministry of the South Louisville Christian Church.

The most emotional part of the morning for me happened during communion.

A teenage boy gave a moving devotional to prepare us to take the Lord's Supper. All the ushers serving were teenage boys, dressed in suits or sport coats and ties. It was interesting to me as I thought about those boys being the leaders at South Louisville Christian Church in a few years.

Worship is important. Communion time is important. Respect for people is important. God is important.

Around me were all kinds of people. Wealthy, poor, middle class, some dressed up, some very casual. African American, White, Asian, old, middle-aged, and lots of youth gathered for a worship celebration.

But the one that stood out to me the most was an elderly man accompanied by his nurse sitting in front of me. He was in a wheelchair. He could not speak, only made sounds. Yet his mind appeared alert. He loved his church, and I heard he went every Sunday morning to a service.

As I picked up the bread and the juice from the tray handed to me, I looked at the man in the wheelchair. His nurse stood up, put her arm around his shoulder, and placed the cup of juice to his lips. It took three different times before he finished the one tiny cup of juice. His nurse patted his mouth with a tissue after each swallow. She whispered to him, dabbing again and again.

My eyes flooded with tears as I ate the bread and drank from my cup. What a picture of hospitality and servanthood, of compassion and love shown to this precious man by his loving nurse. A perfect example of the compassion of Christ as we all met around His table.

CHAPTER 28

Mishaps in the Kitchen

"Let no corrupting talk come out of your mouths, but
only such as is good for building up, as fits the occasion,
that it may give grace to those who hear."

Ephesians 4:29, ESV

AT THE MOST inopportune times, disasters happen in the
kitchen. Regardless of whether you've dropped a pan of mashed
potatoes or forgotten an ingredient, it's not the end of the world.

Floor Potatoes

Aromas of baked turkey and dressing were filtering throughout
the house. On the kitchen counter were large dishes of corn
pudding, green beans with bacon, and a sweet potato casserole,
piping hot and ready to eat. Our mouths watered as we waited

for dinner. Sometimes sneaking a piece of carved turkey helped the hunger pangs. A shimmering cranberry salad also waited for the first spoonful to go on our plates.

Dinner was ready, and it was time for everyone to gather around the table. I needed to get the mashed potatoes from the oven. I grabbed two hot pads and opened the oven door. The buttery mashed potatoes were staying warm, waiting to grace our table.

As I began pulling the foil pan of potatoes from the oven. I cringed. The foil pan bent and slipped from my hands, landing upside down on the floor.

I yelled for help and Lisa, my daughter-in-law, came to the rescue. Together we picked up the pan of hot potatoes, leaving the top layer spreading out on the floor. Will I be able to fix this mishap? Only moments earlier butter covered the mashed potatoes and looked so beautiful as it melted.

Twenty guests were waiting to get the call. All is ready. This unexpected mishap will need some major attention.

Lisa and I cleaned up the potatoes and butter. Concerned someone might slip and fall because of the slippery spot, we washed the wood floor with soapy water and wiped the spot dry. In case some potatoes touched the floor, I scraped off the top layer and added more butter. Real butter.

No big thing? Easy for you to say. Family folks gave me grace and soon forgot about the near disaster. How would you react if you ruined all those piping hot mashed potatoes laden with bright yellow butter? Cry? I was near the edge of an emotional flare-up. I stayed calm.

I learned a valuable lesson. Never place a flimsy foil pan loaded with buttery mashed potatoes in an oven without first placing the pan on a baking sheet.

We need to shrug mishaps off and laugh. You might have to give up your serving, though, of butter-laden mashed potatoes.

The Salt Shaker Mishap

Guests will soon be arriving. Salt was all over the floor sur-rounding me. I was afraid to take another step as salt stuck to the bottom of my shoes. Great way to start a luncheon. The salt shaker needed refilling, which I should have done earlier, not five minutes before guests arrived.

My friend Sherry, spotted a small hand vacuum in the laun-dry room and grabbed it, whisking all the salt away. I'm grateful for quick thinkers in potentially tense circumstances.

It's times such as this when wonderful friends who work alongside you are a real blessing. Never say no to one who says, *can I help?* On that day, the salt shaker mishap could have been a real fiasco. I can't imagine salt being tracked everywhere.

Cobwebs and a Special Luncheon

Our friend's son, a doctor along with his wife, planned to go to Kenya and work at a hospital. Several of us agreed to host a luncheon and raise funds for this sweet couple. We wanted to help and encourage them on their first mission year. Thirty-four ladies confirmed they were coming and would be of financial help to the couple, too.

We ordered Kroger's Derby Chicken Salad, and my friend, the bread baker extraordinaire, baked bread and brownies. A scoop of mixed fruit and a lettuce leaf holding a scoop of chicken salad was on one end of the plate. We placed the brownie and slice of homemade bread on the other end. Since the plate was rectangular, this worked. We filled the glasses with ice and lemon slices ahead of time and poured the water when guests arrived.

I was confident the unusually shaped white plates I pur-chased from a party store would make a lovely table setting. Apple-green, satin ribbon tied around the program booklet and napkin offered a nice touch of color. We slipped under the ribbon, a sprig of fresh, fragrant thyme. A silver-colored plastic fork, knife, and spoon lay next to each plate.

The centerpieces were white orchids. Artificial white orchids my friend put in an arrangement that looked real. Guests were complimenting them, as they carefully reached to touch the blossoms.

After the lunch, Val, the doctor's wife, told guests about their plans to go to Kenya and work at the Tenwek Mission Hospital.

The luncheon was a success as guests committed half of the couple's financial needs for their first year. We were thankful for the opportunity to honor this young couple.

The guests left, the kitchen was clean, and I sat down to relax. I leaned my head back in the chair on the back porch and took a deep breath. As I looked up towards the corner of the porch, I spotted an old dirty cobweb, a huge old cobweb! I never noticed it when cleaning earlier in the week. Eight ladies sat out there for our luncheon. Oh my, I hope no one saw that awful, ugly thing.

Reminders, though. Regardless of how much time you spend preparing for a party or luncheon or dinner, or how hard you try to make your home perfect, something happens. Yes, your table setting is lovely and the meal, tasty. You may have forgotten something and realized life is never perfect. Even on the back porch.

Guests Want Our Attention Not Our Perfection

If someone asks, *will you be willing to host an event*, I take about two seconds and say, we can. The word no isn't in my vocabulary when it comes to entertaining people.

The crisis pregnancy center asked if we would host a luncheon at our condo. Yes. However, saying yes can bring some tense moments in preparation.

Their invitation list was extensive, and we needed to plan where to seat everyone for lunch. My list of things to do was getting longer and longer. I was squeezing this event into our already overcrowded calendar.

My To-do List:

1. Find someone who could direct guests for parking.
2. Place online order for 35 "Nothing Bundt Cakes" miniature cakes a week prior. They package the cakes in a round clear-plastic bowl with a lid. It will be easy to eat the cake from the bowl or take home for later.
3. Ask gals to come on Thursday to set the tables.
4. Buy four dozen plastic plates, cups, silverware and napkins.
5. Pick up flowers for tables on Friday from Whole Foods Market.
6. Write out place cards and name tags. Place name tags in alphabetical order on the credenza.
7. Make a seating chart for guests seated at different tables; lay place cards out.
8. Set out ice coolers, buy sparkling cucumber water and an assortment of teas.
9. Order the Qdoba taco salad and trimmings.
10. Hang up clean towels in bathrooms and clean counters and toilets.
11. Have extra toilet paper and tissues in the bathrooms.
12. Fluff pillows on the sofa and straighten the great room coffee table.
13. Set out plates, tablecloth, silverware, etc. for the back-porch table to prepare for the luncheon the next morning.

14. Turn on lights and candles throughout the condo and
    adjust the temperature.
15. Sweep off the front porch.
16. Schedule cleaning for the condo a few days prior.
17. Borrow drink dispensers from neighbor.

I scheduled four appointments for the day before the fund-raiser. Not very smart. Stressful, for sure!

As I was driving to my second appointment, my cell phone rang. "Mrs. Russell, this is Anna from Qdoba." Qdoba was catering the lunch, and we decided on tacos for the luncheon, since there would be men and women attending. Thinking we wanted something fun, tasty, and easy to serve.

"We are sorry, but the caterer should have told you when you booked your order. We can't leave our store until 10:30 a.m. It's a store policy."

Stammering, I said, "But they promised me someone would come to set up and leave by 10:45 a.m. I've got over 30 guests arriving before 11:00 a.m."

"We do not have a driver available. I've called two other stores and they have no one either."

My mind was racing. Could I pick up the food, drive home, and set everything in place? Before guests arrived? Hmm.

"You can pick up everything that you will need," he said.

I wanted to say, *the reason I scheduled your store to deliver and set up was because my time was tight.*

Instead, I said, "Do I get my delivery fee back?".

"Oh, yes, we will credit your delivery fee."

We agreed. I would have someone pick up the food at 10:25 a.m. sharp on Saturday morning.

I put out an SOS text to the 3 gals helping me. Tina,

my sweet neighbor, texted me and said, "I will pick up the food".

I sent a text back, "Oh, bless you, dear one". Yay for people who say yes!

Two hours after my appointments on Friday, I was to meet Bob and some friends for dinner. I checked over my list of things to do before morning. The front porch needed sweeping.

As I stepped outside, there was something weird-looking on the porch floor. A dried-up pinecone, perhaps, as I kicked it aside on the porch. With a jolt, saying out loud, "What is that? A mouse? A dead baby mouse! How did that thing get on our porch?"

Something drug that mouse onto the porch. A cat or dog? Dogs are on a leash in our neighborhood. I don't recall seeing any cats. Sometimes we see wild animals wandering across our neighborhood lawns. Did a possum or raccoon bring the mouse to our porch?

Guests want our attention rather than our perfection.

My mind was racing with thoughts of how many people stepped on our porch and a dead mouse was lying there?

I stood motionless, wondering what to do. Tina's husband, Don, popped from around the corner. He was delivering the iced tea jugs and drink dispensers for our luncheon the next day.

I asked him, "Did you notice something strange on my porch?" He looked puzzled as he shook his head and said, "No."

I pointed to the floor. "It's a dead baby mouse."

"What are you going to do?" Don asked.

"Well, I could throw it under our bushes, or in the woods. I might get a plastic bag and throw in the big trash can. What do you think?"

He said, "Put it in a plastic bag and throw in the trash." Then he said four words. "Grab me some pliers."

"Pliers? You want a pair of pliers? What will you do with pliers?"

Imagining in my mind, *is he cutting it into pieces?*

He said, "I'll throw it in the woods."

Oh, please Lord, let there be pliers in the toolbox in the garage, as I hurried to look. Our toolbox isn't your typical red metal box. You know, the kind that has a top that flips open, showing an assortment of carpenter's tools? Ours, instead, is a shoe-sized plastic box, and the lid doesn't even fit tight. I might find a lady's hammer, a few tiny nails and one or two little screwdrivers, and a pair of pliers.

Ah, I found the one-of-a-kind Russell toolbox and inside was a pair of pliers. I handed the pliers to Don and turned around to walk back into the house. I didn't want to know where the dead mouse landed. But very grateful our neighbor stopped by just in time and offered to get rid of the unsightly creature.

This entire experience showed me I needed to learn to pace myself. Check my calendar and not plan so many things for the day before a major entertaining event. Life throws unexpected curve balls. So, take a deep breath and persevere.

The important thing is to consider who will walk through your door. Pray for those on the guest list.

Guests want our attention rather than our perfection.

Everyone enjoyed the luncheon and fellowship and the best part? Guests pledged over $140,000 as seed money for the crisis pregnancy fundraiser dinner.

This fundraiser was a blessing, mouse and all!

Kind Words are like Silver Boxes

Potted yellow and coral begonias were at each place setting as a thank you gift. I was having a luncheon to say thanks to a group of friends who helped wrap and pack my good china and dishes for our move. It would be a simple lunch, lovely and fun.

I set the table with my yellow, black, and white china and black-handled stainless-steel silverware, stemmed goblets and sunshine yellow napkins. It looked special.

I ordered six orange-glazed salmon filets from a market about 15 minutes away. I shopped often at this market and knew the salmon would be perfect.

It was the designated pickup time. "I'm sorry," the deli manager said. "There has been a mistake. We don't have enough of the orange-glazed salmon for your order." The order was two filets short.

I stood, stunned. "Oh no! I need 6 pieces and five guests are coming in an hour and a half and I'm placing the salmon filets on a bed of lettuce for each lady."

The filets were not big enough to cut in half and share.

He responded, "I'm sorry. We can call another store and you could pick up there."

"I live fifteen minutes from this store and further away from the other stores. There is not enough time."

He shook his head, "I'm sorry, but someone didn't place the order in the precise manner."

Someone said the six salmon pieces would be ready when I got there and I needed something. Another worker said, "A truck is coming within the hour. The driver has extra salmon filets."

I calculated in my mind to go home with my items, change my clothes and come back; there just wasn't enough time. We were to eat at 11:00 a.m. It was now past 9:30 a.m. I was thankful everything at home was ready.

"What do you suggest I do?" I had bought food to serve with the salmon. Thinking maybe they have something else I could use instead of the salmon.

I asked, "Do you have chicken breasts, six of them?"

The deli manager said, "Since it is our mistake, I will deliver the salmon to your house myself. Where do you live?"

"You would do that?"

A lady employee chimed in and said, "I'm going home in an hour. I don't live far from you and I will bring them to you." I wanted to leap across the counter to hug her.

She saved my day by extending the hand of hospitality to me. A gracious example of great customer service.

Instead of me saying, "I'm never shopping there again", I'm saying, "I will shop there again!"

The lady from the deli brought the salmon filets as promised. Something else I didn't expect: she warmed the salmon filets, ready for the salad plates. Perfect timing!

I was so thankful that I kept my cool with the deli manager and didn't say something that would come back to haunt me. Sometimes it's hard to speak gracious words.

To stay in a state of calmness can be difficult. Where would it have gotten me if I had blown up and shouted and demanded the extra salmon filets? They were not even in the store.

In those kinds of circumstances, I am reminded of a book I read years ago called *Silver Boxes*,[26] by Florence Littauer. The book told how to gift others with words of encouragement. Mrs. Littauer writes, "When our words come out of our mouths, they should be like little silver boxes with a bow on top, ready to give away."

Think about that. We are to speak words of kindness and encouragement as a verbal gift in little silver boxes .

Fire and Smoke

We moved to our new condo a few days earlier and several friends stopped by to help unpack boxes. Thankful for their help, Bob picked up a Chick-Fil-A sandwich for each person's lunch. I put them in the microwave to keep warm. Oops!

It shocked me to hear a strange popping and crackling sound from the microwave. I forgot the sandwiches came packaged in bags with a foil lining.

Flames suddenly shot up inside the microwave, which wouldn't have happened had I used the regular oven. Not having used that microwave yet, I couldn't find the cancel button. An eternity passed.

I finally found the open-door button and threw a glass of water on the flames. People stood around dazed and jabbering.

The fire alarm blared with a loud, piercing sound. Well, at least we know it works.

Yelling, "Open the doors, we need to get the smoke out."

When opened, they caused a draft that pulled the smoke out. All was well. No burnt sandwiches, and the foil bag protected them from the water. No damage done, except my pride.

Whew! Welcome to our crazy home.

CHAPTER 29

Between North and South

"They are to do good, to be rich in good works,
to be generous and ready to share."

I Timothy 6:18, ESV

COMMONPLACE HOSPITALITY EXPRESSIONS in the south are an
upbeat *good morning* and *hello*, *thank you*, and *how can I help?*
I love the showing of kindness and being courteous to people.

These words are not heard as often in the Midwest. I grew
up in the corn-belt country of east-central Indiana. My home-
town was Orange with not a single traffic light. There was one
tiny grocery store, two churches, and the township school that

housed all twelve grades. The school gymnasium was the largest in the county for a township school.

My two younger siblings, a sister and brother, rounded out our family of five. We walked to school, played outside, and rode bikes up and down the streets of town. A favorite pastime was playing in the sandbox and playing hopscotch on the sidewalk.

I loved our tiny town. My daddy was a rural letter carrier and my mother, a homemaker. Our modest home with its big front porch sat behind enormous maple trees. Massive vegetable and flower gardens were at the back of our house.

Hospitality was an important trait in our family, people came often. I've wondered if my parents grew weary with so much company. Instead, those visits energized them. My dad was a genuine people-person, and it thrilled him when people stopped to visit.

Things got polished, mopped, and swept clean if we knew ahead of time that guests were coming. Baking finished, tablecloths and napkins made ready, and the menu planned. The meal included fresh or home-canned vegetables from the garden. A vase of flowers sat on the table in summer months.

There would always be plenty of food to feed hungry preachers, missionaries, and anyone else who stopped by at dinnertime. The warm welcome and gracious hospitality shown by my parents rubbed off on me. I think God was preparing me to marry a preacher.

People stopped to tour the rose garden in summer's cool evenings. We grew accustomed to unexpected guests.

I learned how to grow flowers and plants and share them with others. My dad taught me how to care for the roses and flowers. I learned to plant peas, carrots, corn, tomatoes, green beans, and potatoes. My favorite thing to do was bite into a juicy red tomato, pulled from the vine and warmed from the sun's rays. It was sheer joy to have a saltshaker in hand and red juice dripping off my wrists.

My daddy picked flowers, along with fresh vegetables, and wrapped them up for guests to take home. There were lots of red plump strawberries, purple grapes, and in the fall, delicious juicy golden pears to share. I remember the pear tree producing baskets and baskets of pears. We gave pears to trick-or-treaters, who came by on Halloween night. They stood in awe with that rare, ripened fruit.

I joined the 4H club when I was nine years old. Members learned how to bake, sew, can fruits and vegetables, cook, entertain, and organize a home. Each member kept a journal explaining what they did and how it turned out.

4H members entered items to compete with others at the fair every summer. We might get a blue ribbon on the entry, if lucky. A blue ribbon means the entry met lofty standards. You were state fair bound if awarded a purple ribbon, which meant superior standards and quality.

I got so excited when I entered my chocolate cake and was awarded a blue ribbon. To my dismay, it cracked in the middle and fell open on the plate. The judge said, "Your cake was delicious. It deserved a purple ribbon. But I couldn't give you one because it split and wasn't perfect." It disappointed me. It was good, although not perfect.

Older 4H members served as junior leaders, teaching cooking and baking skills through visual demonstrations at club meetings.

One year, I did a *How Not to Bake a Cake* demonstration in the firehouse meeting room. I was thankful for the concrete floor, because flour had gone everywhere. White flour was on the table, the floor, and me. Members were in hysterics. How did I pull off that demonstration? We didn't have the Food Network as an example. I was on my own and appreciated the training in baking I received from my mother and our township 4H club.

I began taking piano lessons when five years old. One year

the church needed a piano player for the worship service and as an 8th grader, I became the church pianist until graduation from high school. My world seemed to become unique.

My third year of college, I discovered that God's plans differed from mine. I met a young man studying to be a preacher and fell in love. Not at the top of my to-do list. My plan was to major in classical piano performance and be a concert pianist. And the rest of the story?

Bob and I lived in the country near the church he pastored when we were first married. I wasn't an excellent hostess. Working my full-time job at a brokerage firm in the city, I would come home dragging and too weary to prepare for guests.

Our first home of four rooms, with one small bathroom, was tiny. The rooms were 12 feet by 12 feet in size, but we managed. Family and friends visited often, and a homeless man spent a night.

I needed advice to be better at hospitality. I should have paid closer attention to my parent's example. (1 Peter 4:8-10 NIV) reminds us we are to show hospitality without grumbling. Regardless of whether we are hosts for a large or small group or an individual in our home, we are to be friendly, personable, sympathetic listeners, gracious, calm, and flexible.

I tried to improve my hospitality skills by watching the hostesses in homes we visited. My observation of their calmness and graciousness or how uptight they were with guests was very helpful for me. I like everything near perfect and would wonder if the hostess wanted us in her home.

It was the practice at the small church that someone would take the preacher to their house for lunch.

One particular Sunday morning, we overheard an elderly lady talking as she checked over the list posted on the bulletin board. It was her turn to feed the preacher and his wife.

We knew it stressed her when we heard, "I didn't know I had to have the preacher today. I have nothing prepared." This puts one in an awkward position. We tried to encourage her not to worry, no problem. We preferred going home and spending the afternoon relaxing.

Our hostess insisted we come for lunch. I wondered what she would find to eat. Not your typical lunch! It was a huge salad of fresh-picked endive, a bitter-tasting plant used in salads. An unusual lunch, with unexpected hospitality, but memorable.

I remember this unusual meal and researched endive. Endive has a crisp texture and slight bitterness that can give a pleasing flavor to a salad. Sorry, but I'm not an endive fan.

That Sunday morning, I shall never forget watching sheer determination unfold. I'm certain the dear sweet lady spent most of the worship hour wondering what to serve the preacher and his wife? It was a great lesson reminding me to not worry. Everything will be okay.

We have lived in Louisville for over 56 years. It is considered the south, and we've truly enjoyed being here. Yet, after all these years, I'm still learning about hospitality.

I'm not the perfect hostess. My preference is to have things perfect and pretty and planned out. Things are seldom perfect and pretty and planned out, except in a magazine. I guess we could light candles and only entertain after dark if the house needs cleaned.

Do you think of yourself as the perfect hostess? And what is your greatest concern? People seated at your table or the menu? Weary from cleaning the house before guests arrived? Feeling the pressure as a "hostess-with-the-most-est"?

I catch myself and am convicted, because Scripture commands us to be hospitable.

Even though I grew up in the north and learned hospitality from my parents, I have thoroughly enjoyed living in the south, an area where folks are welcomed with open arms that show warm southern hospitality.

CHAPTER 30

And the Door Opened Wider

"For the word of God is alive and active. Sharper than any double-edged sword, it penetrates even to dividing soul and spirit, joints and marrow; it judges the thoughts and attitudes of the heart."

Hebrews 4:12, NIV

IT WAS NEARLY twenty years ago when I first met her—a lovely young lady named Gala.

She and her family immigrated to America from Ukraine a few months earlier. Her first job was greeting customers at the door of the spa I visited each week. She became fluent in the English language and is now a licensed esthetician.

I sit across from her every other week getting a manicure. It took a while to understand words spoken with her Russian/Eastern European accent. Sometimes she looked up a word in

Russian for its meaning. We talked about holidays, children, foods, and the unique traditions of her homeland and America.

Gala knew my husband was a minister, and she took an interest in what we were doing. How was our weekend, our family?

Gala is a wonderful lady and I love her dearly. But she was reluctant to talk about church and spiritual things. Then one day she explained why. When local government officials discovered people were going to church, they might send soldiers to kill members of the family. That could have been her father. It sickened me hearing those words. We in America take our freedom to worship for granted. For Gala, soldiers would possibly kill her father if their family attended church.

Her grandmother told her stories from the Scriptures. I ached for Gala, prayed for her, and invited her to church.

One day I gave her several of Bob's sermon stories with biblical applications on CDs. She listened, because she told me about the stories. I gave her devotional books and books for her twin girls.

Not giving up, I asked Gala and her husband to go to our church's annual Easter Pageant. Nothing to fear. The church members used drama and music to portray the life of Christ. I was thankful to extend her the opportunity to attend. She talked with her husband and they agreed to go with us. Not knowing the effect on Gala and Alec, I prayed for God to open their eyes and ears to Jesus' message through drama. They loved the pageant.

When checking with me on dates for the pageant that next year, she wondered if they might get tickets for her brother and his wife. Now Gala was inviting people. I made a mental note to get four tickets to give to them. It thrilled me they came several years, along with other employees from the spa.

One day, Gala asked me to pray for her father who was sick. I wanted a quiet place. She asked me again as I was about to leave. This urgent ask was unusual. I didn't care what people might wonder. Gala needed me then. I wrapped my arms around her and whispered a prayer in her ear. We pulled apart, and with tears in her eyes, she thanked me.

I told Bob about her asking for prayer, and we talked about having Gala and her husband for dinner one evening. And why not invite Bob and Kathy too? Their ministry supported an orphanage in the town near where Gala used to live.

Kathy and I talked, and we decided on a girls' lunch instead. We met at a pleasant restaurant, and the conversation turned to Ukrainian food. Kathy traveled to Ukraine often and enjoyed the food served there.

I lifted a prayer in my thoughts. This idea is incredible, Lord. You have brought us together at a table and food is the one common thread that is bonding us together. A wonderful picture of being open to God's command to practice hospitality.

Although I knew both ladies, I didn't realize how great their love was for the food in Ukraine. Before we finished eating, Gala said, "Let's do this again and next time, come to my house and I will fix a Ukrainian meal."

We set a date on our calendars. The door of gracious hospitality was opening wider as we fellowshipped around the table.

Several times we met at each other's homes for lunch. We talked about family and food and church. On one occasion, Gala taught us how to make Russian Pelmeni Meat Dumplings. We rolled out dough for dumplings and spooned ground beef onto the bite-sized circles of dough. Then we pinched the dough together, formed a half-moon shape, and dropped the dumplings into the pot of boiling water on the stove. Oh my, so good and we ate lots.

Jesus met unfamiliar people for a meal around a table. A meal together was the perfect place to listen and learn from Jesus. I love conversations with friends around a table.

I often mentioned my Bible study and what we were studying.

One day Gala asked, "What is a Bible study?"

"My Bible study is a group of women that meet every week at church. A lady teaches from a book in the Bible. We will discuss parts of that lesson around our table. Six other ladies study together at my table. I call it my Bible Study Table Group. Come and go with me? We meet on Tuesday mornings and we finish at 11:00 a.m. You will love meeting my friends. And you know JoAnn."

Before she even spoke, I realized her answer. She worked Tuesdays, and the spa was closed on Mondays.

So, I offered to meet with her on Mondays and study together. And we did. She told me before our first lesson, "Judy, I'm a blank white piece of paper," as she held her hands out. "I know nothing!" Chills ran up and down my spine. The door was opening wider for learning about Jesus.

I chose a seeker Bible study book by Becky Pippert, *Spirituality According to Jesus*[27]. When we met for the next-to-last lesson of our study, I asked her this question. "Gala, tell me what touched you or moved you with this week's study. What stood out to you?"

She paused and said, "I now realize that Jesus is the Messiah."

I still get chills thinking about her words.

After finishing the Luke study, she asked to do more. I regret we can only meet every few weeks because of her work schedule, but we continue to study together as often as possible.

We tried meeting several places. Then we went to our church and met in one of the compact living rooms provided. I liked the quiet, small, uninterrupted space. We grabbed a quick bite in the coffee shop and then started our study together.

I decided instead of sitting on soft chairs a few feet from each other, why not sit at a small table? It was easier to talk. We were used to discussions at her manicurist table. It surprised me how enjoyable it was to lay our books out and open our Bibles and study at the table opposite each other.

I wanted a Russian Bible for Gala. My son Rusty has a Russian small group meeting at his church and they got me one. I had given her an NIV Bible earlier. It thrilled her to have both. She looked up passages in her Russian Bible that helped her better understand a particular verse.

We completed the book, *The Women of Easter*[28], by Liz Higgs earlier that year. Now we are working on Warren Wiersbe's study, *Be Rich*[29]. This study is from the book of Ephesians and shows us the riches we have in Christ.

"For it is by grace you have been saved, through faith." (Ephesians 2:8, NIV). We receive the gift of the Holy Spirit who lives in us at baptism. That is our spiritual armor to fight the enemy's attacks and have the promise of eternity with God, our Heavenly Father, and Jesus Christ.

Gala's twin girls were attending Vacation Bible School at a church and were interested in what their mom was studying. She began reading to them from *Be Rich*. She shared God's word with her family.

Isn't it incredible how God works things for his glory? A lunch, a Bible study, and a table. Only God knows the outcome of life for Gala. But my prayer is that she accepts Jesus as her Lord and Savior, and that we can continue studying together.

The three couples have met several times for dinner, and I continue seeing Gala for a manicure. We talk about Bible studies, current events, family and the desperate times in her country, Ukraine, and in America. I stand amazed seeing God's hand in this. It shouldn't have surprised me, because it started with three ladies eating lunch together around a table and sharing life. Hospitality around the table.

CHAPTER 31

My Grieving Friend

"The Lord is close to the brokenhearted and
saves those who are crushed in spirit."

Psalms 34:18, NIV

I SPOTTED HER sitting on a bench outside the Fireside room at church. The Sweet Spirit Singers rehearsal started in a few minutes and we met there. "Hello, how are you? I'm Judy Russell."

The young lady responded with an air of joy and happiness. "Hello, I'm Gwen. I brought my kids to youth group tonight. We started coming here to church."

"As long as you are here, come join our group of Sweet Spirit Singers? Our rehearsal is beginning soon."

She jumped at the chance.

I watched the ladies, it thrilled me to see them welcome her with open arms. I was proud of each one.

Years earlier, I formed the Sweet Spirit Singers ladies choral group. We met on Sunday evenings, and worked hard practicing three-part harmony to sing at church and in nursing homes. Those 40 singers loved the Lord, people, and singing. We prayed for each other, laughed, and sometimes cried together.

What a thrill to have Gwen join our ladies.

Gwen's life wasn't easy. A single mom, she raised her children and worked a forty-hour-a-week job. Still, this lovely Christian lady overflowed with grace and joy.

Then Gwen met Mike at our church. They dated, became engaged and married, and started volunteering in their Sunday Bible class and other ministry areas. This couple was a blessing to our church family. Gwen, a talented organizer, also helped me with our women's ministry program.

A visit to the doctor's office brought devastating news. Mike faced a vigorous and deadly cancer with only weeks to live. It was a tremendous blow to their family and our church family. Mike died a few weeks later.

I couldn't imagine the hurt and agony my friend endured. She was being comforted by her strong faith in Jesus Christ. But what can I do for her? What can I say? I felt God nudging me and invited Gwen to come to our house for lunch.

A family favorite, tuna sandwiches, was easy to prepare. A can of tuna, chopped apples, and crushed walnuts, mixed together with mayonnaise. I scooped the salad onto two whole-grain toasted bread slices. Then added chips and grapes to the plate. Choices of soda topped off our lunch that day.

We ate out on the screened-in porch, a quiet place with a light breeze blowing. There were no bugs to bother us, and colorful birds singing added a refreshing touch.

I listened as Gwen shared her recent weeks. We talked and laughed, cried and prayed, and nibbled on food. It was healing for both of us. A grieving release for Gwen and a blessing for me.

We sat around the table for several hours. Four, to be exact. My friend needed a listener, and I'm thankful to have given the gift of precious time. Other things could wait.

Gwen and I still get together for lunch and an occasional girl's overnighter. I still remember the first time I met her. Did God place her in my life as an encourager and friend? I think so.

Hospitality isn't always food and parties, but giving of your time, love, compassion and a listening ear.

What to Say to a Grieving Friend

Sometimes it's difficult knowing what to say, or how to help. It's hard for me, too. Check the ideas below for help with ministering to those dealing with grief when visiting with them.

1. Say, "I'm so sorry."
2. Tell them you will pray.
3. Hug them and say nothing.
4. Relay a special memory, only if proper.
5. Keep your time short, maybe 5-10 minutes.
6. Plan to get with your friend weeks later.
7. Call and check on them in a few days.

When you've made Christ the center of your life and home, his love will shine through you. That is Biblical hospitality.

CHAPTER 32

Hospitality and Making Memories with Grandchildren

"Be very careful then how you live—not as unwise but wise,
making the most of every opportunity, because the days are evil."

Ephesians 5:15, 16, NIV

ONE DAY OUR 6-year-old grandson Chapman was riding with me in the car. "Nana, how old *are* you?"

Chuckling, "I'm 72." That was several years ago. He is 15 now.

He was quiet for a few moments. "I think you will live to be 82. And you can watch me grow up."

Our grandchildren have their entire lives ahead of them. We grandparents have more days behind us than before us.

Paul writes to Timothy, "I am reminded of your sincere

faith, which first lived in your grandmother Lois and in your mother Eunice and, I am persuaded now lives in you, also." (2 Timothy 1:5, NIV).

Lois had taught her grandson Timothy the scriptures about Jesus. Paul says, "Timothy had a genuine faith."

The faith of Lois has been an impressive example for grandparents and parents. Remember, we all have a responsibility to pray, teach, and train those under our care. Our days are short and evil lurks in every corner.

Have you ever considered treating your grandchildren like you would a best friend who visits? You have things cleaned up, extra snacks, time set aside for fun things, an enjoyable meal prepared. You look forward to the time together.

We often overlook the "nice" things for our own family. They are more deserving than someone just popping in. They love us like no other.

The Thanksgiving Blessing Jar

Our Thanksgiving tradition at the Russell's is the Blessing Jar. It is a small round pottery jar filled with multi-colored corn. At mealtime, we pass the blessing pot around the table. Each person picks out a kernel of corn and tells what they are thankful for during the past year.

"We look forward to it every year," our grandson Charlie said. "Every once in a while, when my wife Faith and I reflect on how God has blessed our lives, we turn to each other and say, 'blessing jar!'" They were planning to share how God has blessed them that year at our family Thanksgiving gathering.

Christmas Any Day

Since Bob and I are not the only grandparents to our grandchildren, we decided it was okay sometimes if we celebrated

Christmas on a day different from December 25. We can enjoy opening gifts any day. It's how we perceive it that counts. If we make it exciting, they will be excited. If we relax and enjoy, they will be relaxed.

Our Christmas tradition before opening gifts is to read the Christmas story and pray together. It helps to remind us of the reason for the season.

It's sometimes difficult deciding what to give for Christmas gifts when children get older. In Nancy Sleeth's book *Almost Amish,* she writes: "Instead of buying a bunch of gifts for each person, buy only three; one spiritual, one educational and one for fun."[30]

I enjoy buying books and games, plus something for fun. The first year I did this, it was as if someone had lifted a load off of my shoulders.

One year for Christmas, I gave each grandchild an age-related book on manners. That was their educational gift. (wink) Easy to find when shopping on Amazon!

Easter Time

The most important thing we do at Easter is worship together at church. But I love doing fun traditional things like coloring eggs.(Chapter 14) For our Easter egg hunt, I resort to colorful plastic eggs. To keep it fair, I prepare ten eggs per child. They each have one color. We put coins and bills in the eggs and hide them in the house. No weather worries.

One year, I received a text from Charlie on Easter Sunday night saying, "I miss you all, I want to go on an Easter egg hunt!". He was 23 years old.

Try a tradition of sharing the Easter story with Resurrection eggs. We fill the Eggs with items that tell the story of Easter. You can place them at each place setting on the Easter table and have the children tell the Easter Story as they open up their egg. Find the Resurrection eggs at your local bookstore or make your own. https://www.faithward.org/diy-resurrection-eggs-for-holy-week/31

April Fool's Day Pranks

I can be a trickster. I've short-sheeted beds, placed roving eyeballs on food in the kid's lunch boxes, and one of our favorites—fake brownies. Yes, I painted different sized wooden E letters brown. Thus, Brown E's! I put the letters in a cake pan and covered them with a sheet of brown construction paper along with a note, April Fool's. But don't disappoint them. Have another pan filled with warm brownies.

"A cheerful heart is good medicine, but a crushed spirit dries up the bones". (Proverbs 17:22, NIV)

Encouragement and Sports

Over the past 50 years, I've gone to at least a million sports games of my husband, sons, and grandkids, including practices. It's a chore sometimes, but when you see them glancing up in the stands to see if you are there, it's worth the effort. Go to their games, even if they sit the bench.

Special Birthdays

For the Russell grandchildren, the 10th birthday is special. We take a special trip with only the birthday grandchild. Nana and Pop choose the trip and it must be historical. Afterward, I make a trip photo album just for them. They love it.

Most of us can't take elaborate trips. But a weekend a hundred miles away will be fun. The important thing is doing something. Your own city is probably full of museums, art galleries, and nature parks.

One at a Time

Make a point of spending time with each grandchild by themselves. Go out to lunch or breakfast, to the park, shopping, fishing, playing golf, or a tearoom. It's a special time to ask questions and talk one on one.

A Library of Children's Books

I pulled our sons' old books out of storage and put them on shelves. I also bought recently published children's books from the church bookstore. The grandkids would climb in bed with a stack of books to read. They loved finding books with their dads' names inside the front cover.

Grandchildren's Memories

To prepare for this book, I asked the grandchildren to write some of their memories. Imagine my surprise to get these comments from our now oldest grandson, Charlie. "I'll always remember how you knew to make things special. Even in the insignificant details. You would put our names at our spot at the table or write a message on the chalkboard. There were candles on the table and cute decorations for the holidays. It was like a magazine photo."

Those details are work, but it is proof that the extra work makes those times memorable. We know that time with family is a special and valuable thing. Those are treasured memories I will cherish forever.

Favorite Family Dinners

Charlie writes, "I remember lots of family get-togethers when we ate Snow on the Mountain. We would celebrate being all together as one big, lucky family."

Our granddaughter Corrie says, "I remember those Saturday nights after church when we would watch a U-of-L game at Nana and Baba's. The smell of turkey chili filled my nose and I hear Nana or Baba's voice in the back of my mind. It comforts me and I am thankful for such joyful, wonderful childhood memories.

Corrie and her cousin Kimberly would ask, "Can we set the table fancy?" I enjoy having a lovely table. What a perfect opportunity to teach where the silverware and the glass and napkin go.

Camp BaNanaPop

Camp BaNanaPop became a fun tradition with our grandchildren. I'm called Nana, they call Bob, Pop. But Corrie calls him Baba. Thus, *Camp BaNanaPop*. Our boys, Rusty and Phil, would call and say, "Do you have time for Camp BaNanaPop? We need a break." We take two or three days and go to local museums, historical homes, nature sites, learn to bake, grocery shop, and all kinds of things to learn. It's fun.

Take Photos and Text Them

If your grandchildren are 15 and under, they have grown up in the digital world. They've always had the iPad and smartphone. So, get your smartphones out and start clicking away. Otherwise, you are missing out.

Celebrate When Grandchildren Marry

Our Granddaughter-in-law, Faith, shares about visiting in our home.

"The first time I visited Nana's house, I was engaged and wasn't even married to Charlie yet. She immediately made me feel like I had always been her granddaughter.

In fact, the reason I was visiting Louisville was because she was throwing me a bridal shower with all of her dear friends, whom had never met me. It was one of the sweetest, kindest gestures I'd ever received.

Every detail of that bridal shower was so beautifully thought out. I had never felt so loved by my soon to be grandmother-in-law and from strangers I had just met.

The minute I arrived in Louisville I was treated with the kindest hospitality. As I walked into Nana's house for the first time I was greeted with a "Welcome Faith" message on her cute bunny whiteboard decoration.

In the guest room there was a water pitcher and granola bars for a snack or early breakfast and I remember that striking me as such a thoughtful detail to do for guests. Of course, the room and her entire house was decorated beautifully and felt so inviting, warm, and cozy. Nana's house quickly became a place I loved to visit and where I felt right at home.

One thing I look forward to about visiting Nana's house with Charlie is that she often caters in a meal. I was introduced to a Kentucky favorite at my bridal shower and quickly came to love it— the Kentucky Hot Brown!

She also has a whole shelf of board games and Nana and Pop always take the time to be intentional and play games with us when we visit. She's even introduced us to some new board games we love playing.

Some of Charlie's and my favorite memories are of just the two of us visiting them and sharing lots of laughs, playing games in their warm, cozy house and enjoying Kerns Kitchen Derby Pie or Graeters ice cream—two more Kentucky favorites Nana introduced to me that I now love."

Surprise Them Sometimes

Plan surprises, something unexpected, like ice cream after football practices. It might become a tradition you look forward to during the summer.

I will never forget this surprise idea that came to me for six-year-old Johnny. Rusty and his family moved to Florida that summer and it was now fall. Fall in Florida isn't like fall in Indiana and Kentucky. Johnny missed jumping in the leaves that fell off the trees in their yard and always raked into a pile. Our six-year-old grandson asked, could we go home to Nana and Pops, so I can jump in the leaves?

Now my mind started swirling. Maybe I could send him some leaves? I got some heavy-duty yard bags, filled them with leaves, packed them in a gigantic box, and shipped them to Florida. Johnny could now jump in the leaves. I wondered what their neighbors thought.

Pray! Pray! Pray!

Pray that each child accepts Jesus as their Lord and Savior. That was one of my many prayers answered for my grandchildren. Each one has accepted Jesus and been baptized. Both families are faithful to the Lord. We are blessed.

Spending the Night

Grandson Andy wrote, "My favorite thing about a sleepover at Nana and Pop's is the unexpectedness."

Unexpectedness! I like that word, don't you? There would always be something unexpected happening at our home.

Andy continues. "One night we would play a board game, other nights we might watch Gilligan's Island. We would always have a Bible story that Pop would read to us. Then Pop would ask questions, and we would have to answer. When we got in bed, if it was the entire Russell group of cousins, Pop would come into our rooms and scare us. My two favorite times were when he was a witch and put an adhesive bandage on his nose and wore Nana's garden hat and rode a broom. Another time was the headless horseman. Nothing special, he just put his jacket over his head. We laughed for a long time."

Can you imagine Bob dressing up like that?

Kimberly writes how she remembered taking a bath in the big tub, putting on her PJs, and then going downstairs to the kitchen to eat cookies and have the Bible story. "We gathered around the kitchen table and listened to the Bible story. Pop would ask some hilarious questions about the story, testing us after reading."

Tommy remarks, "I have countless fond memories of staying with Pop and Nana. From board games to Nana's famous cookies, it's always fun. Every night we stayed with them Pop would read us a Bible story before bed. I'll always appreciate him teaching us about God since before I can even remember."

Charlie remembers, "Every night I was at your house, before bedtime I would get a cookie, a glass of milk, and Pop would sit down and read us a Bible story. That was a special and powerful memory for me. I listened to Pop read the stories of the Scripture simple enough for a six-year-old to understand and a

25-year-old to remember. That helped to build a solid foundation for me, even more than I realize."

Chapman says, "I always love the cookies that we make, and playing games, and reading Bible stories at night. Everything is always so clean and ready for us to stay."

Did you notice something? Two threads ran through the grandkid's notes about spending the night. Bible story time and chocolate chip cookies! It wasn't trips or gifts or surprises. It was the simple things. Like warm chocolate chip cookies and a glass of cold milk.

Important things like reading a Bible story and praying before bedtime. Hospitality with grandchildren and beautiful memories around the table at the end of the day.

Grandchildren Call You Blessed Too

When I celebrated my latest decade birthday, our children and grandchildren spent the evening with us. We ate dinner, enjoyed cake, opened gifts, and celebrated our time together. One of my gifts was a precious homemade "book" by our grandson Johnny. Especially precious because he was 17 years old, and boys don't usually make books for their Nanas at that age.

His book, titled "10 of the Many Reasons Why I Love Nana," also represents the many reasons to invest in our grandchildren.

1. Nana has impeccable hospitality. She's even written a book on the subject.
2. Nana loves to spend time with us. She learns new games to play and activities to enjoy.
3. Nana prefers grandson Johnny over grandson Andy. She clearly said that Andy is her "second most favorite 17-year-old grandson." (Oh, the competition between cousins!)

4. Nana is the youngest and prettiest 80-year-old I've ever seen.
5. Nana is by far the world's most tech-savvy 80-year-old She owns more Apple products than anyone else in the family!
6. Nana is a thoughtful gift giver. It may be Pop's money but it's Nana who comes up with the thoughtful, creative gifts.
7. Nana is incredibly supportive and adoring of Pop. Nana is a great role model for how to be a loving spouse.
8. Nana is proud and supportive of all her children and grandchildren. She shows up to sporting events and sermons.
9. Nana makes us cookies. Forget all the other reasons! This is the one that really matters.
10. Nana loves Jesus. She has modeled how to be faithful over the course of a lifetime.

CHAPTER 33

Bible Stories Around the Table

"From infancy you have known the Holy Scriptures, which are able to make you wise for salvation through faith in Christ Jesus."

2 Timothy 3:15 NIV

STILL ON A bookcase shelf in our home is the Bible storybook my dad read to me when I was a young child. I remember crawling up on his lap to listen as he read God's Word written for children. I was excited when I could read those words myself.

Our first child Rusty was not even a year old, and we started reading stories to him from a tiny Bible story picture book. He loved hearing us read.

We wanted a book suitable for little children and found one by Kenneth Taylor at the local bookstore. *The Bible in Pictures for Little Eyes*[32]. Ironically, the rectangular-shaped book included the same Bible story pictures that were on my elementary Sunday school lesson leaflets.

I searched Amazon, and the older version is still available in used condition. An updated version is now available. This little book has all the rich stories we shared with our sons.

Following the boys' bath time, we would read from the Bible storybook every night. We prayed and thanked God for the day, each other, our friends, and relatives.

We asked God for wisdom, direction, and protection for all four of us. Story time included snacks, glasses of milk, and a plate of homemade chocolate chip cookies. Rich moments for the four of us around the kitchen table.

Something special happens when a family gathers around the table in meaningful conversation.

Sometimes the boys' friends needed prayer. Conversations were about church and community programs they were struggling through. There were talks about their sports teams at school. It disappointed them how they played or didn't get to play. These were important times to share.

Today our boys have similar conversations with their children. They include us when we visit.

We carried on the tradition of reading the Bible story and having prayer time together until the boys left home for college. When they came home for a break, we prayed, and read Scripture together until they married and moved away.

Over the years I would buy new Bible storybooks and devotionals for the boys. It was fun taking a new book from the shelf to read for our nightly devotions.

Later, God blessed our family with grandchildren. It thrilled me to get the Bible storybooks out again.

Our seven grandchildren gathered around our kitchen table with glasses of milk and homemade chocolate chip cookies to hear a Bible story and pray. Pop asked questions to see if they listened. It could become a serious matter if they didn't have an answer. And if an answer was wrong? There was teasing and laughing.

Our grandchildren are teenagers and college students now. We still read scripture and pray when they come to visit and spend the night. Glorious memories are still being made.

"At that time, the disciples came to Jesus and asked, 'Who, then, is the greatest in the kingdom of heaven?" He called a little child to him, and placed the child among them. And he said: "Truly I tell you, unless you change and become like little children, you will never enter the kingdom of heaven. Therefore, whoever takes the lowly position of this child is the greatest in the kingdom of heaven. And whoever welcomes one such child in my name welcomes me."

Matthew 18:1-5, NIV

CHAPTER 34

Ready for Interesting Guests

"Give thanks in all circumstances; for this is
God's will for you in Christ Jesus."

I Thessalonians 5:18, NIV

OUR CHURCH'S LIVING Word Bookstore was humming with
customers wanting to buy books and tapes. Across the hall,
tape ministry staff scrambled to reproduce tapes of speeches and
workshops. I was rushing back and forth between the bookstore
and tape ministry, greeting conference attendees.

It was our church's annual leadership conference. Pastors,
their ministry staffs, and other church leaders traveled hundreds
of miles to come and attend workshops, hear great messages,
and take part in meaningful worship services.

The time of preparation is long and tiring. The planning is stressful for the entire church staff. But it is rewarding to meet people, listen to questions, and give them something to take home to their church family.

Early Friday morning, Bob called me to say he was playing golf with Max Lucado that afternoon. I knew Max was at the conference and brought several of his leaders, but didn't know he was playing golf with Bob.

Later, I arrived home and as I opened the door into our house, Bob calls out. "Judy, we have company. Max is spending the weekend with us."

I walked into the family room, finding both guys slouched on the sofa with feet propped up on the coffee table still wearing their golf hats.

"Well, hello Max."

Mind you, I'm overwhelmed at this point with everything else that is happening; and now I'm hosting Max Lucado?

Laughing, he said, "Bob invited me to come. Last night I didn't sleep. The guy sharing my room snored loud and kept me awake."

Chuckling, "I understand. I'm glad you are here and can rest."

So thankful to have rooms ready for guests, even if they are unexpected ones.

I rushed upstairs to the guest bathroom and switched out the hand towel and checked the sink and commode. Everything was in good shape.

I peeked in the first guest room. The queen-sized bed with a yellow matelassé spread and wide painted stripes on the walls in yellow and white looked great. It may be my favorite room in our house. Black and white buffalo checked pillows with yellow cording, dust ruffle, and window valance, softened the vibrant yellow. Perfect for guys and gals.

When we redecorated the room, I emptied the closet and

dresser to make ready for guests to place their belongings. A small desk and chair are ready for study time or letter writing and a large oblong footstool is perfect to lay open a suitcase.

Twin beds graced the second guest room. I decorated each bed with a red paisley duvet cover, white pillows and dust ruffles. We used this room for grandchildren who often spent the night.

Dozens of children's books lined the shelves of the enormous bookcase. I piled stuffed animals on the beds. Others were in a large fabric box beside a small rocking chair. The red bedroom was a perfect spot for grandkids to nap or sleep. Although, I'm not so sure about a grown man. It, too, is always ready for guests.

Max came back to visit several times. Sometimes he brought his agent and said to him, "That's my room," pointing to the yellow room. You can have the red one. We always looked forward to those times when Max called and said he was coming to town.

We were fortunate to have rooms for overnight guests.

A Sultry July Night

In Kentucky, the middle of July is always hot.

Thank you, Lord, for air conditioning. On this sultry day, we planned to celebrate our son Phil's 42nd birthday. Rusty and his family came into town, and this would be a fun family time together.

Earlier, Phil quipped, "Mom, I don't want to celebrate my birthday with guests here."

I'm a flexible person, but from his perspective, not this time. Who, me not flexible? Did I listen to Phil? Ha, ha. I'm his mother. Sometimes you need to listen to your heart.

Over the years, we've celebrated Phil's birthday in some rather out-of-the-way places. We've celebrated in hotel rooms, on vacations, church camp, picnics, in a hurry, and a few years, at home.

In July 2013, the North American Christian Convention met in Louisville, and Phil's birthday was the same day the convention concluded.

Since I organized the women's events that year, I invited Liz Curtis Higgs and Ann Voskamp to speak at our ladies' sessions. I felt responsible for their weekend in our city.

The Bible says, "make the most of every opportunity", (Ephesians 5:16, NIV) and this was a perfect occasion to invite them to come to our house for dinner. So, even though Phil's preference would be not to include guests for his birthday, what a special time for grandchildren to be exposed to Ann and Liz, two famous Christian authors, blog writers, and speakers. So, I seized the chance and invited Ann and Liz for dinner and to celebrate our son's birthday.

Our family has known Bill and Liz for years. And Phil introduced me to Ann Voskamp's blog. This would be a great evening for our family.

We served dinner and enjoyed conversation around the table. After singing happy birthday and eating cake and ice cream, Bob said, "Let's gather in the family room. I've asked our special guests to share their testimonies with our grandchildren."

This announcement came as a surprise to me and I'm thinking, why not? Let's go for it.

The kids raced to the family room, as if expecting something unusual. They sat cross-legged in a row on the carpeted floor. Bob invited Liz to speak.

She stood. "Is it okay to tell the gory details, too?"

The kids ranged in age from six years old to thirteen. And Liz included the gory details.

Liz was serious and funny. She relayed events of her past life with men, alcohol, and drugs, leading up to the time she gave her life to the Lord.

As Liz shared the dramatic change in her life, our grand-kids sat wide-eyed, listening to every detail. God has used Liz and her remarkable story to reach thousands of people. We are proud of her.

Then it was Ann's turn. She stood. "I prefer getting closer to them."

She gathered her skirt around her legs, dropped to the floor, and sat cross-legged, just a few feet in front of our grandkids. That got their attention.

Again, they listened as this servant of God told her life story of struggles. Ann grew up on a farm. She battled depression and watched as a delivery truck accidentally ran over and killed her baby sister. God has used Ann, through her speaking and writing, to touch many lives, too.

I didn't see our grandchildren move the entire time Ann and Liz spoke. It may be years before they realize the uniqueness of that evening. To have two of the most talented and sweetest Christian women sitting and talking one-on-one with them was a rare occasion. We all received a blessing.

That year, I volunteered as the chairperson and coordinator of the women's conference for our convention. Even though everything went well, conventions are hectic and stressful. And hosting guests for dinner was not at the top of my priority list.

To be honest, I got up that morning thinking what have I done? I don't even remember what we ate. An ice cream cake? A catered dinner? I determined to make that evening special for everyone, and I needed any help I could get. So, I ordered dinner.

The important thing was for Phil to have an enjoyable birth-day celebration. And the second most important thing was to open our door with smiles and greet our family and our special guests.

The benefit of entertaining guests in your home is the impact they can leave on your children who are growing up. Guests don't need to be world-famous. Churches often ask for volun-teers to host visiting musicians, teachers, preachers, speakers, or

Bible college students. An evening or meal with them can affect your children in a positive way.

I've heard Bob recall as a young boy when the Vernon Brothers quartet ate dinner at his home. They helped him milk the cows! That exposure to likable Christian young men contributed to his decision later to enter the ministry.

It thrilled us to host special guests that evening for Phil's birthday celebration, even though we were weary in doing good. God still blesses times of exhaustion. He gave us the extra energy to go forward and do something special for Phil, our guests, and our family.

As I look back, I remember that July night with fond memories. The evening turned out to be one of the most interesting and heart-warming gatherings I can ever remember hosting in our home. I am thankful for the time together, with elbows on the table, celebrating a birthday and relating memories with special guests.

And Phil later admitted he really enjoyed the evening.

> "Give, and it will be given to you. A good measure, pressed down, shaken together and running over, will be poured into your lap. For with the measure you use, it will be measured to you." (Luke 6:38, NIV)

Old Friends

My friend Elizabeth called me, talking so fast I barely understood a word. Dick and Becky Pippert Molenhouse were vacationing in the same Florida condominium complex as Elizabeth and John. Becky had asked her if she knew me, and the rest is history.

I wanted to reach out, so I made a phone call. We had become acquainted years earlier when I invited her to speak at our church for a women's event. But this call was not an invitation to speak, but to come and visit. It was good hearing her voice.

I said, "We would love for you to come for a visit?" I so wanted to get reconnected.

Yes, Becky and her husband Dick, will come visit us and stay a few days.

The doorbell rang, and I raced to the door. Oh, my goodness, how wonderful to see her. We hugged and greeted each other like old friends.

One evening Becky came downstairs. "I forgot the blouse I need for my suit to go to church tomorrow. Do you have something I might borrow?"

"Let's go check my closet." We found the perfect piece.

Guests often forget things when traveling. Items such as a toothbrush, hair spray, or even a piece of clothing. Our hospitality from the moment guests come through the door will give them a clue that they can ask for help. I'm sure you've forgotten something you needed when away from home. It is embarrassing to ask for help.

We've loaned guests shirts, dresses, shoes, scarves, skirts, and even a tuxedo.

One night we were hosting a party and a couple who came were to go to a formal event later that evening. Susan recounts the story:

> "The Living Word Ministry's Christmas Party at your home was lovely—the people and the food, everything. We needed to change clothes for a black-tie event downtown. You were gracious enough to offer your upstairs primary bath for us to change clothes. However, Ron realized he brought only his tux pants, shoes, shirt, and bow tie. He left his tux jacket at home. In typical

Judy (and Bob) genuine hospitality, you pulled out Bob's tux and loaned Ron his jacket to wear that night. Ron still loves telling that story."

I am so thankful they were not afraid to ask, "Could I borrow?" They returned the jacket, cleaned, and pressed. Blessings returned from hospitality.

Girlfriends Overnighter

It was our granddaughter, Corrie's 17th birthday, and she was eager to celebrate with two of her best friends. They just so happened to be the governor's daughters. The twin girls had been in school with Corrie since first grade.

She asked if they could stay overnight at our house. It thrilled me to get her call.

Bob and I were out of town, so Corrie's mom stayed with the girls.

I assumed they all slept in the walkout lower level. There were two sofas in the family room along with several large air mattresses in the closet. A big screen tv and many board games and a bumper pool table to have for entertainment. Also, another guest bedroom and a full bath.

After we arrived home, we discovered they didn't stay on the lower level, but upstairs on the main level. Corrie's mom slept in the guest room and the three girls slept in our king bed in the primary suite.

Hmm. Maybe I should put a gold plaque on the door saying "Governor's Twin Daughters Slept Here?" It's historical, don't you think?

Corrie and the girls had a fun overnighter at Nana and Baba's. We are grateful our home was a welcome place.

I was so thankful I put clean sheets on our bed before we went out of town. We've had our sons and their wives spend the night if there was a storm and they had no electricity. I try to always have beds ready. Thankfully, the sheets are clean.

It is important that your home be a place where family can come anytime. I am honored when grandchildren ask if they can celebrate their birthday and bring a best friend to our home.

Hospitality is the opportunity to show people you love and care, even if you are not there.

CHAPTER 35

The Blessing Jar

Give thanks to the Lord, for he is good; his love endures forever.

1 Chronicles 16:34 NIV

I LOVE THANKSGIVING Day. It's a special time when families join for a big turkey and ham dinner, watching football games, playing table games with family, and taking naps. We all expect to stuff ourselves full of comfort food and desserts.

Our family gathers to give thanks for the past year and remember the blessings received from God. It's the perfect time to give thanks for our freedom of worship and living in a country like America. What a wonderful holiday to celebrate with family.

In Gloria Gaither and Shirley Dobson's book, *Let's Make a Memory*[33], they share a unique way of showing thankfulness at Thanksgiving by having a blessing jar. I wanted to do one.

I found a tiny round pottery jar that was perfect. I filled it with kernels of multi-colored corn representing blessings. We have passed that little jar around our Thanksgiving table for over 35 years—tables in Kentucky, Pennsylvania, Ohio, Indiana, Tennessee, Florida, and even Hawaii.

I begin the tradition by taking a kernel of corn out of the jar and handing the jar to the person on my right. They take a kernel of corn and the jar continues being passed around the room until everyone has a kernel.

I pick up my kernel of corn and share my blessing for that year, placing the corn back in the jar and guests continue passing the jar around the table. We each tell what we are thankful for during the past year. Everyone does. Old and young alike. There is laughter and tears, along with the usual family teasing.

The boys and Bob still humor me about that tradition, but I know they've been thinking about what they will say for several days prior.

One time when Rusty was away in college, he called my parent's home about the time he knew we would do the blessing jar. He wanted to share his blessing with our family.

We used to do this tradition before we ate, but our family grew larger and it took longer. So, we now have our blessing jar tradition after the meal.

Those kernels of corn in our jar hold many blessings from years gone by. Our jar is set on a bookcase shelf in our kitchen. Visible every day as a reminder of God's goodness to our family and the countless blessings shared at Thanksgiving time.

Topping the list of blessings are weddings, grandchildren's births, job promotions, graduations, and kids' baptisms after accepting Jesus as their Lord and Savior.

It's a great moment for families to remember and express

thanks with words of God's goodness. Why not start a Thanksgiving family tradition? Plan a time to be thankful around your table with friends and pull out your blessing jar.

Happy Thanksgiving.

CHAPTER 36

Expressing Hospitality in Different Ways

"I can do all things through him who strengthens me."

Philippians 4:13, NIV

WE CAN EXPRESS hospitality in many ways. Not only around a table eating a meal, but with words of encouragement, friendly manners, a smile, and a wave.

If there is a need to help or serve a neighbor or friend, show hospitality with acts of service. Offer to help mow someone's lawn or do their laundry. Cook a meal for the family with a new baby.

I know a lady who loves doing laundry and has helped her pastor and his family by doing their laundry for them.

Extend hospitality to people with an invitation for dinner or dessert in your home. Ask neighbors to go with you to church or a Christian play.

Offer to host college students or speakers visiting your church and make a space for them to sleep. Just think, Jesus didn't have a home of his own. He stayed with families the years he traveled and taught.

A Picnic in a Field

It was always an enormous meal. Golden brown chicken, fried to perfection. Buttered, sugary sweet corn on the cob. Sliced, juicy red and yellow tomatoes. And always rice or beans. Home-canned applesauce was on the menu too. Homemade bread and churned butter with homemade preserves or jam. A fruit pie with a homemade crust and baked that morning for dessert. My goodness, nothing better. That was hospitality on the farm.

I can remember my grandmother and my Aunt Mary preparing those enormous meals at noon for hired hands and family during the planting and harvesting months. There was always an abundance of food and leftover food from the noon meal the family ate that evening.

Their noon meal was called dinner, not lunch, as we say today. Farm people work very early in the morning and need food to restore energy for their afternoon hard labor. Thus, they had dinner at noon. Their evening meal they called supper.

I met a lovely 87-year-old lady named Mrs. Thomas at a church where Bob was speaking. She and her husband own thousands of acres of farmland. The family continues working the land today.

I said to her, "Did you feed the farmhands lunch while they were working the fields?"

"Oh yes, I always fed them. In fact, if they were working the fields five or six miles away, I went to them."

What? I had never heard of this. Intrigued, I asked her, "You took food out to them?"

"Yes, I loaded up a bucket of water." Winking at me, she said, "They need to wash up before eating. I packed dishes of food, a square folding table, and loaded everything into my car. Then, I drove several miles to the field, set up the table, and laid the food out so the men could eat.

"One time a salesperson was driving by and saw me and stopped. He asked me what I was doing. "I'm preparing dinner for the workers."

Stunned, he said. 'I've never seen this.'"

Mrs. Thomas continued on, "I have an extra plate. You want to join us?"

WOW! That's unusual hospitality to invite a complete stranger for dinner in a field.

I later found out this was a common practice for a farmer's wife whose husband owned many acres of farmland. But having a picnic in a cornfield? That is hard to picture.

You can have a picnic anyplace. In your backyard, the middle of the family room floor, in a city park, and from the trunk of your car. A picnic along a mountain stream can be beautiful. Try having one on your porch or office desk, and yes, even in a cornfield.

Lay a tablecloth on the family room floor one snowy afternoon and have a picnic of baloney sandwiches, chips, and soft drinks, or peanut butter and jelly sandwiches. Serve cups of hot chocolate and warm cookies. The children will love the surprise picnic.

First Responders Party

We needed a service project for our Bible study group. How about doing something special for Louisville police officers? Why not take snacks to the district police stations in Jefferson County? A gracious way to say thank you to the officers for keeping our city safe. Since it was near Halloween, we gathered bags of candy and snacks to distribute to the police stations in our county. It made for a grand party, a thank-you time.

My table group wanted to go to Police Headquarters in downtown Louisville since my son was the Public Information Officer. I checked with him and he agreed.

Phil wanted us to use the conference room adjoining his office. This was a perfect place to set up our treats.

"Blessed are the peacemakers, for they will be called children of God." (Matthew 5:9, NIV)

Our group decided to set up a buffet table with all kinds of snacks and desserts. We spread out a fall-colored tablecloth and laid out napkins and plates making a lovely table and the treats more appealing. I picked up a bouquet of mums to put on the table for a centerpiece. Many people think men never want flowers. But I've discovered, they do. It is a pleasant surprise to see flowers on a table just for them. An act of hospitality to our first responders.

The ladies brought apple cider to drink, along with some soft drinks. There were chocolate chip cookies, a peanut and candy corn mixture, pumpkin bars, and brownies for the officers' snack time. We brought the food in throw-a-way containers and left everything not eaten with the officers to snack on later.

We gathered in a circle and prayed for them, thanking them for their work to keep us safe and appealed to God to protect them as they protect our city.

We spent about an hour showing hospitality and encouraging people we didn't even know, hoping to show how much we appreciate the time they have given to serve us.

Why not ask your Bible study or small group to consider a service project such as this? A morning of hospitality.

"Blessed are the peacemakers, for they will be called children of God." (Matthew 5:9, NIV)

Staff in our Whirlpool Tub

Our two sons and their wives asked questions as we stumbled over our words to answer and tell stories. We just arrived home from our two-week mission trip to Kenya and Mombasa, Africa.

So thankful to walk into our brightly lit home and drink clear cool Louisville water. We have to do without sometimes to appreciate everyday things. Things such as ice cubes, good water, clean floors, and bright lights. As we stood around the kitchen island, a weird noise came from the bathroom above us. Is that the whirlpool tub running?

We raced upstairs, discovering three of Bob's staff in the whirlpool bath tub! They wore shorts, t-shirts, and held unlit cigars. They pretended to be startled and exclaimed, "Oh no! We thought you were coming back tomorrow night!"

And to top it off, they appeared to be drinking wine. Stunned at first glance and puzzled at how they got in the house, we began laughing hysterically.

Even though it was an unusual way to welcome us home, their greeting was endearing. We were glad they felt comfortable enough to think of the idea. Our son was in on it and let them in the house.

A party or a meeting or even an unusual surprise will bind the team together. Had they not been accustomed to being in our home, they would have been uncomfortable being there that evening.

Progressive Dinner Party

I like progressive dinners, because the host handles only one part of the dinner instead of a four-course meal. Part of the fun of a progressive dinner is visiting in different homes and tasting interesting foods.

One of my favorite progressive dinners we hosted happened around Christmas time. About 50 of us—all pastors and their wives from Southeast—rode in a rented school bus. It was the best solution for traveling to the different points. Everyone met at church. The last stop was our house.

We made four stops: appetizers, salads, the main course, and then dessert.

I asked our son-and daughter-in-law to dress up in Colonial Williamsburg style costumes I rented from a costume store. The Colonial couple greeted guests at our front door. Phil even held a Musket, and they both looked like an authentic colonial couple.

Our home was decorated for Christmas. A wreath of fake fruit hung on the front door, and candles were aglow in the windows and throughout the house. The Christmas tree sparkled and freshly cut pine branches gave the house a smell of Christmas.

Everyone was laughing and enjoying the evening. They started coming through our front door and found something quite unexpected at their senior minister's home. Even Bob looked at me, wondering *what has my wife come up with this time*. I had conveniently not shared my plan with him. I enjoy doing surprises for parties, and this one had a surprise.

A gal we knew started a business called Hillary's Cafe. She would go to businesses and people's homes and serve guests gourmet-styled coffees.

Tall bottles with flavored syrups were in place beside coffee machines on our kitchen island. Dozens of clear glass coffee mugs sat in a row on the kitchen table. Guests drank 2, 3, 4 cups of flavored coffee. Hot chocolate, too. It was the most fun party I ever pulled off! I actually did it a couple more times.

At another progressive dinner, the guys would sneak a lamp or chair from the couple's house where we stopped earlier. When the evening came to a close, they began bringing items inside, asking the group, "Who does this belong to?" As if they didn't know.

To this day, I don't know how they got a lamp and chair off and on the bus with no one seeing. But that progressive dinner will long be remembered.

I enjoy serving desserts, as guests get to linger longer and dessert is not rushed. It is a more relaxed time and people can spread throughout the house or gather at a table.

Dinner guests can be your neighbors or a group of friends from across town. Neighbors could walk to each other's homes. If friends gather from across the city, why not rent a bus or do a van parade?

Try a Progressive Dinner some evening with your small group or class. End the evening with singing around the piano and playing Name That Tune.

Bananas with Greetings

Each one had a handwritten note on the bright yellow skin. "Have a Good Day". "Smile". Mine read "Good Morning Sunshine."

What a clever way to give a morning greeting. We were staying overnight at the Hampton Inn in Port Charlotte, Florida, and I had gone down for their complimentary buffet breakfast. There, stacked in a basket, were several small bananas with greetings for guests.

I thought, wouldn't that be fun to have delivered to your guest's room on their breakfast tray? Or placed on the breakfast table? Maybe even stick in your kids' lunch box to give them a word of encouragement when they open their school lunch box. Or your husband's if he carries his lunch to work.

Try a scripture verse, or "I love you", or "Merry Christmas", or "Happy New Year." Words to brighten someone's day found on a banana.

CHAPTER 37

An Introduction to Hospitality for the Younger Guests

"Children's children are a crown to the aged, and
parents are the pride of their children."

Proverbs 17:6, NIV

I BOUGHT A child's china tea set to use with my three-year-old
grandson, Charlie. You are wondering, tea with a boy? Well,
let's not call it tea. Why couldn't a small boy do lunches with
his grandmother, using tiny teacups and plates?

I remember our two sons drinking from tiny little plastic
cups. We didn't do tea parties, but had lunch or cookies and
milk from toy dishes. A perfect time for encouraging words and
teaching while having a child's party.

Children love pretending, and a perfect choice of food might be Nana's chocolate chip cookies and a cup of milk. So, why not have an afternoon snack with miniature teacups?

A friend gave me two old child-sized library chairs. She thought they would be perfect for my grandson. And they were. I often pulled them up to our coffee table. I decided one day while keeping Charlie; it was the perfect time for a snack. So, I laid a kitchen towel on the end of the coffee table and covered it with a napkin. The tiny teacups and saucers fit on the large napkin I placed on the table.

Little triangular-shaped peanut butter and jelly sandwiches and cups of milk were the perfect choice for a boy's snack. Tea and scones weren't the order of the day.

The two of us sipped from tiny cups and ate tiny sandwiches. One-on-one time with a grandchild sometimes merits creativity. Such as snacks at Nana's in the middle of the afternoon. I'm not sure Charlie remembers the "tea party," but I will never forget our time together that day.

What a perfect opportunity to pray for your child or grandchild. Pray in front of them and for them. Pray out loud, saying their name. Pray for specific things about them. Eating and praying together is showing hospitality to a child.

A friend gave me a tea set to use with our grandchildren, with the theme from the nursery rhyme, "Peter, Peter Pumpkin Eater." The set included little cups and saucers for four people along with a creamer, sugar bowl, and teapot.

Sometime later, I found a child-sized handmade oak table and two little ladder-back chairs at an artisan's fair. When I pulled all four child-sized chairs up to the table, it made a perfect meal place for grandchildren. Meals with Nana and Pop or Mommy and Daddy happened often.

All seven of our grandchildren pulled up a chair and sat at that little oak table. We have used it many times—eating snacks, enjoying meals, playing games, coloring pictures in books, and sharing tea parties. Yes, tea parties! Sometimes with tea or a soda, milk, or just plain water.

There were many tea parties at that little oak table. Some were real and some pretend. Each one full of laughter and lessons learned. The perfect setting for hospitality with a child.

A Little Girls Tea Party

My most memorable little girls' tea party was when Corrie turned six years old. She and her mom wanted a tea party. A *real* tea party.

The birthday party day finally came. Little girls in pretty dresses looked adorable as they arrived.

Corrie's daddy wore a suit and tie and met each little girl as their parents pulled up in the driveway. He opened their car door and escorted the little girls into the house. Phil was their very first escort; how touching is that?

This tea party was not with toy dolls but was the real deal. Real cups, real saucers, real petite tea sandwiches, real tea, and real sugar cubes.

I carried several hat boxes to our music room. My hat collection provided several stylish choices. The little girls tried on hats, pranced around, and pretended to be fashion models as they squealed and giggled.

Then it was teatime. The five-and six-year-olds gathered in the dining room and Phil helped them with their chairs. Little tea sandwiches to savor and tea in china teacups for sipping. Each girl loved picking out cubes of sugar and dropping them in their hot tea. It fascinated them as they watched the sugar cube melt.

I enjoyed observing the young guests. This tea party was not with toy dolls but was the real deal. Real cups, real saucers, real petite tea sandwiches, real tea, and real sugar cubes.

There were small slices of cake on individual pedestal cake stands. A glass-domed lid sat over the cake. The small stands were placed at the left of each guest's place setting.

The little girls seemed nervous. Did their mommy say to be careful? Don't drop, spill, or break anything? I think Corrie's mom and her aunts were nervous too.

But I enjoyed every moment. What if something spilled or dropped? It would have been an accident. Not a big issue.

I will never forget preparing and planning a special tea party for my six-year-old granddaughter. The table full of precious little girls celebrating a young friend and cousin's 6th birthday was perfect.

Colorado Rocky Mountain Picnic

This mid-July day in Colorado was perfect for a picnic. Close to Vail, a park with picnic tables, mountain streams, and trails bid us come for the afternoon. Breath-taking views of wildflowers filled the mountainsides. The clean mountain air was refreshing as we took deep breaths. Bright blue sky and billowy clouds lifted our spirits. We found a lovely spot with a picnic table set in the warm sunshine.

Picnics can be a time of coming together and relaxing.

Shade from the trees made it cool even in July at 8,000 feet above sea level. The warmth of the sun was like comfort food in the wintertime. As we enjoyed our weeks' vacation with our two sons and their wives and grandson, we were blessed with making countless memories.

Remnants of snowdrifts were still under the trees. Snowball fights in shirt sleeves looked weird, but to our grandson and his daddy, it was an unforgettable moment.

A big baloney sandwich, along with chips and cookies in the Rocky Mountains, meant fun in Colorado. That picnic hit the spot!

We hiked, took photos, climbed rocks, and forded streams. When we lapped up the cool mountain water from cupped hands, it reminded me of the story of Gideon in the Old Testament.

"The LORD said to Gideon, 'With the three hundred men that lapped (to lap up the water in cupped hands like a dog), I will save you and give the Midianites into your hands.'" (Judges 7:7, NIV)

What a perfect day.

A picnic with family is fun, regardless of where you go. When our boys were little, I searched under our sofa cushions for loose change, yielding a couple dollars. Enough to buy a liter of soda and a bag of chips. Peanut butter and jelly sandwiches were the main entrée. The perfect ending? Homemade chocolate chip cookies, still warm from the oven.

When Rusty was a little boy, he loved to "throw rocks in the water". So, we chose the park with a vast lake and picnic tables around the edge. Perfect for a quiet evening with family.

Why don't you invite some friends and extended family to a park for a special outing? Your children will enjoy playing with friends.

Sometimes, though, I think an intimate family picnic is needed. Just you, your husband, and your children. Family times are necessary and important.

Are you ready to plan a simple family picnic?

A Graduation Party

It delighted me when our granddaughter asked to have a party at Nana and Baba's. I love having parties at our house. Corrie was graduating from high school and wanted to have an open house dessert party for friends and family.

She and her mom planned, hunted, and gathered ideas and supplies for the party. She hoped to have white hydrangeas and peonies to decorate the rooms. It disappointed me to tell Corrie that the season for white peonies was over. But I discovered white hydrangeas were prolific in our flower shops. I called and ordered several stems and picked them up the afternoon before the party.

They found pink peony cocktail-sized napkins online. The clear plastic dessert plates, glasses, and forks came from the party store. Perfect for this occasion.

Corrie requested a large crystal bowl with huge fresh strawberries for party guests. Since she grew up in Kentucky, Derby Pie would be the dessert. A family favorite. They also filled a tall glass dispenser with icy water, floating lemons, limes, and orange slices.

Since Corrie would start classes in the fall at Samford University in Birmingham, Alabama, her favorite drink was a must-have for guests—Alabama's Milo iced tea. Many guests favored that tea, too.

Corrie designed and made signs for the different areas of the party area. There were food and drink selections and her life history with photos. We tied balloons on the mailbox with the graduation year, 2018. She wrote "Congratulations" on a blackboard easel beside the front door.

Corrie took several photos from her growing-up years, attached them to a white string with teensy tiny pink clothespins. She draped them across the mantle and bookcases, making it easy for people to view. Extra photos were lying on tables.

The party was a grand success. It was not elaborate or over the top cost-wise or work-wise. It was perfect for gathering with family and friends on a spring afternoon.

Special events need advanced planning and preparation. But going crazy with lots of food, drinks, and extras is not necessary. Consider simplifying your next party. Allowing time to rest before the party will help you enjoy the festivities.

Steps to a Stress-free Party

1. Decide on a budget and theme.
2. Choose a date and location.
3. Make a guest list.
4. Select, prepare, and mail invitations.
5. Identify party activities.
6. Choose the food and drinks.
7. Gather decorations, plates, cups, napkins, and silverware.
8. Happy Party Day!

CHAPTER 38

Dinner Party Extraordinaire

"In a well-furnished kitchen there are not only crystal goblets
and silver platters, but waste cans and compost buckets—some
containers used to serve fine meals, others to take out the
garbage. Become the kind of container God can use to present
any and every kind of gift to his guests for their blessing."

2 Timothy 2:20, 21, MSG

"MASTERS OF DINNER Parties." That is a befitting title for
friends known in our family as Mr. Carl and Ms. Deena. Carl
enjoys cooking. Gourmet cooking is his specialty. And Deena
sets a stunning table.

No awkward or dull moments at their parties. We laugh
lots and sometimes cry and pray together before the evening has
ended. Carl and Deena have a gift of pulling together the right
people to make their dinner parties special.

"Plan your guest list carefully. That is the key ingredient to any memorable gathering." Annie Falk, *Palm Beach Entertaining.*[34]

One unique and fun thing is Deena's selection of questions to discuss on a variety of subjects. She sometimes hides the questions under our plates until later. Or we may draw a question from an interestingly shaped bowl.

We have taken part in several unique discussion times. One time I had a question about the South Pole. I was to explain why the ice was melting there. Huh? I knew nothing. What would I say?

As I began talking, my words were mesmerizing to those at the table. I'm not sure a word I said was the truth. The guests thought it was correct. One thing I do know: God tells in his Word that he will never flood the world again.

"I establish my covenant with you: Never again will all life be destroyed by the waters of a flood; never again will there be a flood to destroy the earth." (Genesis 9:11 NIV)

The meals, Carl and Deena prepare, are five courses and will last at least three hours. As we walk away, we are thinking about what an extraordinary evening with dear friends it was. We love it when we get that call to come for dinner.

> *"Plan your guest list carefully. That is the key ingredient to any memorable gathering."*
> Annie Falk, **Palm Beach Entertaining.**

Carl greets guests at the door. He might wear a chef's hat or don a white coat with a towel over his arm. Deena always looks lovely in a dress or pants outfit. Both are smiling and making guests comfortable and welcome. There will be sparkling water or fizzy juice to sip while waiting for those last touches of dinner.

The food is delicious and always full of surprises. You may think, *a five-course meal?* Yes, it's a tasting experience par excellence! The servings are a perfect size. We are not stuffed, just filled enough. Aside from the incredible meal, the evening is a meaningful and enjoyable time for everyone who puts their elbows on Mr. Carl's and Ms. Deena's table.

Practice Makes Perfect

"Start children off on the way they should go, and even when they are old they will not turn from it." (Proverbs 22:6, NIV)

A few years ago, I decided one of the Christmas presents for our seven grandchildren would be a book on manners written for their age. They ranged in ages from eight to twenty-one. I discovered lots of books from which to choose.

We asked our Masters of Dinner Parties friends if they would do a dinner party for our grandchildren? This dinner party would be a time of teaching fun. Our grandchildren would experience hospitality and enhance their manners. Their first real dinner party experience.

Our friends jumped at the chance to spend time with our grandchildren. The grandkids dressed up, and we reviewed ahead of time how they should act. They knew this evening was something special.

Sitting on the floor in front of the children, Ms. Deena asked each one questions about school, sports, favorite subjects, what they did on summer break, etc. Her gentle spirit helped to ease each one. We caught their eye when they took a deep breath and relaxed as they interacted.

Mr. Carl, the chef extraordinaire, listened to their conversation as he put the finishing touches on the dinner. This was an evening to remember. Ms. Deena took time during the meal to explain the many silverware pieces and their uses and other table etiquette. One example was how you drape your napkin on the chair when you leave the table if you are still eating.

Six months later, we drove past Carl's office and our youngest grandchild said, "I wish we could go back to Mr. Carl's for dinner. That was so much fun. I loved the palate cleanser." Now when does a grandmother hear those words from a grandchild? Only when something unique and memorable happens!

All wrapped into one evening was fellowship with cousins and tasting of interesting foods. Good manners explained and put into practice.

You may not reproduce that same evening, but I am sure you can find a plan to help your family learn manners at the table.

"Start children off on the way they should go, and even when they are old they will not turn from it."
(Proverbs 22:6, NIV)

One evening we did a meal in our dining room with our boys who were in grade school. Not a fancy gourmet dinner, just regular food. We thought they needed a learning experience in manners. Manners like showing them how to hold their fork and use a knife. Don't stuff food in your mouth. Keep your elbows off the table while you are eating. (LOL)

What a bomb! The boys didn't enjoy that night one bit. Neither did mom or dad!

As we discovered that evening, it's not the teaching at one meal that brings success, but every time we have a meal together. We needed to teach and remind our children how they are to behave at a dinner party, as a guest in someone's home, and even at the table in their home. Everyone needs practice, and practice makes perfect.

Manners Every Child Should Know

- Come to the table with clean hands and face.
- Put your napkin on your lap.
- Start eating when everyone else does-or when given the okay to start.
- Stay seated and sit up straight.
- Keep elbows (and other body parts!) off the table while you are eating.
- Chew with your mouth closed and don't talk until you've swallowed.
- Don't make ugly comments about the food.
- Say, please pass the..., instead of reaching.
- Chat with everyone at the table.
- Don't make rude noises like burping or slurping.
- Ask to be excused when finished.
- Thank your host or whoever prepared the meal.
- Offer to help clear the table.

How to Set a Table

Not only should we train our children in manners but we should also teach them how to set a table. Where do you lay the knife, fork, and spoon and the order of plates and utensils when setting the table?

Imagine the word *forks*, and lay the utensils left to right. F equals fork. O for plate (the shape of the plate). K for knives and S for spoons. Ignore the letter R in the word.

Try this trick to remember where the glass is to go. When you hold the tips of your thumbs to the tips of your fingers, it makes a lower case "b" with your left hand and a lower case "d" with your right hand. It will remind you—bread and butter plates go on the left and drinking glasses go on the right.

When we teach these rules and tips to our children at a young age, it prepares them for their future. Whether at school, their job, family gatherings, or anywhere they go, they will remember how to show kindness and respect people and things. When practiced at an early age, this will become second nature to them. Practice makes perfect.

Icebreakers

When you need help to get a table discussion started at your dinner party, try some of these questions. Whether they are young or old, guests will enjoy.[35]

Fun Icebreakers Focusing on Things you Enjoy Doing

1. What was your best and worst job?
2. What's the best vacation you ever took?
3. What's the most recent or favorite movie or book you've seen or read?
4. Tell us about your first kiss with your spouse.
5. What's your favorite town or city in the world? Why?
6. Share with us a recent fun experience.
7. Sing or hum a few lines of a song you love. Don't tell the name. Let those around the table guess.
8. Tell us your first childhood memory.
9. What's your favorite sport or physical exercise you do?
10. What's your favorite dish to cook for friends? And for you?
11. Describe the best museum, play, or game you've visited.
12. What was your worst haircut?

Fun Icebreakers Focusing on your Life Philosophy

13. What's your morning ritual?
14. How do you like to spend a rainy day?
15. Describe your own outlook on life in six words.
16. Can you share one quote or saying you love that keeps you going in life?
17. If you could invite four famous people to dinner, who would you choose and why?
18. If you could replay a fun (or deep or big) moment in your life, what would you choose?
19. What would be a perfect afternoon for you?
20. Describe one past action, big or small, you took to improve the quality of your life.
21. Which person in your life do you most admire? Why?

Fun Icebreakers that Press your Buttons

22. If you were mayor for a day, what three things would you change about your city?
23. Describe your most terrifying time.
24. If you could go back in time and change history, what would you change? Why?
25. What's the most anti-establishment thing you've ever done?
26. What would you do in life if you knew you couldn't fail?
27. If you saw someone getting mugged in the street, what would you do?
28. Describe one time you took a huge leap of faith.
29. What was one unknown experience you tried that was uncomfortable for you?
30. Describe a real-life moment where you stood up for someone or something.

Fun Icebreakers that Show Something New About You

31. Two role models you looked up to as a kid?
32. An outlandish/wild thing you did one time.
33. What's the worst present you ever received?
34. What three things do you love about your friends? And three, you don't.
35. What is your favorite smell? What memory comes to your mind?
36. What's one favorite thing you do by yourself?
37. Share one weird circumstance in your life: at work, personal, traveling, or with friends.
38. Share one thing you didn't understand about the world when you were a kid.
39. Describe an embarrassing moment you experienced.
40. Share a personal fact no one would ever guess about you.

Conversation Starters

1. Tell me about your job or career.
2. What is your favorite book you've read?
3. Ask about their name. Is it is unique, ask if it is a family name?
4. Compliment them on their dress or scarf.
5. Compliment them on their dishes on the table or table setting? Are the dishes family heirlooms?
6. How did the two of you meet?
7. How long have you been married?
8. Where did you go to college? What was your degree in?
9. Tell me about your childhood?
10. Where did you grow up?
11. Tell me about your children? Your grandchildren?

CHAPTER 39

A House Guest in Unusual Circumstances

"Therefore, as we have opportunity, let us do good to all people,
especially to those who belong to the family of believers."

Galatians 6:10, NIV

CARING FOR PEOPLE and helping them acclimate to unusual
circumstances is hospitality, whether in our homes or elsewhere.
Let's say the roles are reversed. Now you are the guest.

Have you thought about how you might react to unexpected conditions?

What about times you have visited homes of friends and family and not everything was in perfect shape? You didn't notice the mess because things are not always perfect in our homes.

We hear horror stories that make us want to stay behind closed doors, never to venture out. But think what we would miss in life if we didn't live somewhat adventurously and find ourselves in some unusual circumstances.

Chickens with Dinner

My freshman year of college, I played piano for a mixed quartet that sang at churches on weekends. Even though an introvert, I enjoyed visiting places and helping churches.

The churches planned for us to lead the morning worship, sing specials, present a concert in the evening, and one from our group would preach the message. We always drove back to school after the evening service, sometimes arriving late into the night.

One Sunday morning, the preacher told us we were having lunch at the home of a grocery store owner and would spend the afternoon with his family. Yay, we were looking forward to some wonderful food.

But an unexpected scene caught us by surprise.

After the morning church service, the quartet and I went to our host's home. The five of us climbed the stairs to the owner's apartment above the store. We pushed open the door, stopping in our tracks, speechless at what we were seeing. Two pet chickens were walking around on top of the kitchen table. Uh huh, the table where we were about to eat!

I grew up with chickens. Chickens lived outside in a fenced-in yard. I didn't expect to see chickens inside a house and never on the kitchen table.

Two hours later, all of us started getting sick. I mean, sick! We canceled our evening concert and started back to school. Pulling over along the side of the road several times. Back on campus, we checked in with the school nurse, and she said these words:

"You all have food poisoning. Where have you been?"

"You wouldn't believe our story if we told you." Recovery came the next day.

I can't imagine how our host family felt. I'm not sure they even knew what happened, as we left so fast.

Today, people are so paranoid about food, me included. One thing I know, whether in someone's home or a restaurant, I watch what I'm eating and where I'm eating.

We enjoyed our time visiting with the grocery store owner and his family. I remember their children wanting us to look at their pets and toys and games. A special opportunity for them to have five college kids come and visit for the afternoon. But for us, it was an unforgettable meal with two chickens as guests.

A Pallet on the Floor

College students who travel for their school are on limited funds for meals. When church members volunteer to be their host, students are grateful.

We've opened our home to college students many times. They might sleep in a bed or on a sofa. The guys might bed down on cots or pallets on the floor. College kids are thankful to just get a few winks of sleep.

It is always enjoyable visiting with young students, preachers, and missionaries.

We laugh when we see people at conventions who stayed in our home. They always mention having warm, homemade chocolate chip cookies for snacking. And maybe playing basketball with our boys.

If you stay overnight in a stranger's house, a hotel, or even a friend's home, remember, not everything will be perfect. Your bed may be a pallet on the floor. I know you prefer being in your own bed but look for the positive in your visit.

Pushing Past your Personality

My sophomore year in college, I sang in a girls' trio. We enjoyed traveling to churches doing concerts and representing our school. A perfect opportunity to meet and encourage prospective students.

Sometimes the host church wanted us to divide up and stay in separate homes. And sometimes, we found ourselves in some unusual circumstances.

On one occasion, I was to spend the afternoon and eat at the home of a farmer, his wife, and their two children. Was I looking forward to those next few hours? No way! I was nervous.

I don't have a sanguine temperament and spending time in a stranger's home by myself would be stressful. Have you ever felt that way?

As we look for the positives, it can be tough. Even though, when you adapt to the worst of circumstances, you will receive a blessing.

I'm quiet and I take a while to interact with people. It's hard work to be outgoing when your preference is to sit and listen. If you are alone, you need support and encouragement from friends. Someone to help keep the conversation going. I've worked hard over the years learning to adapt and change that personality flaw. It's not been easy. If I'm not careful, I can revert to listening only.

But that Sunday afternoon I made a significant change. My heart was pounding. I took a deep breath and began asking questions. Where did you live when a young child? Have you been attending church long? What's your favorite thing about farming?

How old are your children? Where did you go to school? Tell me about these photos? I love your table. Is it a family heirloom? Then the farmer and his wife began talking and asking me questions.

Once I started asking questions, it became easier and lots more interesting. I learned about my host and hostesses' lives. That made me appreciate them even more. People enjoy talking about themselves if the answers are positive. The hosts may never ask about your life. But you can interject a fact or two, and they may start asking you questions.

The afternoon turned out to be a pleasant one. Conversations filled with meaningful questions and words helped us get acquainted with each other. I think God orchestrated that I was to be in their home for a specific reason. He was preparing me for a future I didn't yet understand.

The Attic Pot

Sometimes our trio did a three-night weekend revival service. We would be in charge of leading the music for each service.

One weekend my college roommate and I found ourselves as guests who would sleep in an attic bedroom. There were no steps, mind you, just a pull-down ladder we used to climb up to our room.

Our bed was a pallet on the floor made of two stacked mattresses. The bedding was nice, and big fluffy pillows looked comfortable. Since there was no heat in the attic, our hostess had added lots of quilts to crawl under, keeping us warm and cozy. It was as if I was Laura Ingalls in the *Little House on the Prairie* novels sleeping in the loft of their log cabin.

Across the room was a pot. Uh huh, as in old-fashioned. Our thoughtful hostess thought we might need a bathroom break in the middle of the night. She didn't want us to climb back down the ladder, since there was no light.

I will admit, I didn't want to climb down that ladder in

the dark to go to the bathroom. I didn't grow up with indoor plumbing until I was in 10th grade. But I was used to it then, and I didn't relish using a pot.

Even though our sleeping conditions were not the best, just to be in that sweet family's presence was a treasure. This dear family opened their door, regardless of furnishings and inconveniences of only the one bathroom.

Be thankful for a bed with warm quilts and provisions for taking care of those essentials regardless of where you are staying.

Privacy, Please

One weekend, Bob and I drove to a small town in Kentucky to watch a friend's brother play basketball. The boys' mother fixed beds for her sons and Bob in the upstairs bedrooms.

She prepared a cot for me in the corner of the dining room. There was no bathroom on the main level, so she placed a pot for me beside the cot.

I didn't close my eyes the entire night! I was in the middle of everything. It was as if my bed was on a major thoroughfare. I needed privacy to go to the bathroom and get dressed for bed. What would the morning bring?

I waited and waited until I thought everyone was asleep before I climbed out of bed to use the pot. I slept in my clothes, so I didn't have to worry about where to dress the next morning.

Thankful for hardwood floors so you could hear if someone was coming. Although I enjoyed visiting with this family, I hated the sleeping arrangements.

A Strange Encounter

Yes, when I'm a guest, I lock my bedroom door. Don't you? One year on our annual spring choir tour, my roommate and

I stayed with a family that lived in a lovely house. A bathroom separated our room from their 14-year-old son's room. But no lock on our bedroom door to the bathroom. Was that the builder's design? Somewhat strange to have a teenage boy next door that we couldn't lock out.

We finished taking our turn in the bathroom and crawled into bed, turning off all the lights. As we were lying there, talking about the day and quieting down, we sensed a presence.

I said, "What is that?" And sat straight up to see, standing at the foot of our bed, the host's 14-year-old son.

He said, "Are you awake? Could we talk more?" I think it pleased the boy to have someone to talk with about unconventional things.

Startled and scared, we threatened if he didn't leave and go back to his room, we would yell for his parents. We needed sleep, as we had a big day traveling ahead of us. Thankful that incident didn't turn into a terrible one.

Okay, creativity to the rescue! I crawled out of bed and found a chair that I could prop under the doorknob of our bathroom door. We didn't want to lie awake all-night wondering.

What if? Since that time, I've always locked my door when I am a guest regardless of where I stay.

We enjoyed the visit with that family. But a reminder to be alert in all our surroundings.

Fish and Bears

"Sometimes in the forest, there will be bears after dark." That's what our hosts said as we were preparing for the evening.

A few years ago, Bob and I accompanied friends on a fishing trip in upstate New York and stayed in their fishing cabin. Now, I'm not married to a fisherman, nor do I fish. But we love these two couples and looked forward to an adventurous time.

Their cabin sat at the edge of a crystal-clear lake surrounded by a forest of gigantic ash trees and not a cloud in the bright blue sky. At night, countless stars filled the black sky. Quiet. Silent. The only night sounds were the crackling of twigs from animals running through the forest. The soft glow of oil lamps in the cabin, and the moon was the only light we had available.

Although the lake, wildlife, and forest were a picture of Heaven, fishing cabins with few amenities are iffy. Great for guys, but 'roughing' it was not the consensus of the girls and our preference was a pleasant hotel room.

We each had our own room, but no indoor plumbing. The 'outhouse' was about a hundred feet from the cabin and near the lake. They told us we would need to take a flashlight to scare the bears away after dark. Bears? Bears after dark?

Now, that is right up there at the top of my unusual overnight guest stay list. All of our rooms had a pot.

As I've said, things are not always perfect when you are an overnight guest. I didn't drink any water after 5:00 p.m. that evening in hopes that I wouldn't need to get up for a potty break.

Ha! So much for not drinking water or a soda after 5:00 p.m. I found a bright white spot on the floor. and I knew it was THE pot. No way will I get my stiff body to squat down on that low, tiny pot. So, I picked it up, stooping to use it and hoping not to make any noise. Oh, yikes! It was reverberating and striking the side of that metal pot.

I crawled back in bed not to awaken Bob. I knew he was only pretending to be asleep, as he said, "Were you able to go?"

I thought, 'you've got to be kidding me.' The bears outside could hear me. I'm sure I awakened the other two couples.

We started laughing and couldn't stop. Oh, the memories of being a houseguest, even in a fishing cabin. We still laugh about roughing it and cooking fish for dinner.

These stories are not to scare you off from being an overnight guest or hosting overnight guests. Each one is a real, laughable, and memorable story in my life. I don't want to experience them again, even though our hosts were hospitable and full of grace.

We are so spoiled!

Then Jesus said to them, "Suppose you have a friend, and you go to him at midnight and say, 'Friend, lend me three loaves of bread; a friend of mine on a journey has come to me, and I have no food to offer him.' And suppose the one inside answers, 'Don't bother me. The door is already locked, and my children and I are in bed. I can't get up and give you anything.' I tell you, even though he will not get up and give you the bread because of friendship, yet because of your shameless audacity, he will surely get up and give you as much as you need. (Luke 11:5-8, NIV)

CHAPTER 40

Hospitality to Those Outside Your Home

"Do not forget to do good and to share with others,
for with such sacrifices God is pleased."

Hebrews 13:16, NIV

THERE ARE MANY opportunities to be kind and hospitable when we are dining out in restaurants. How can we show hospitality to a server? We can greet them by saying their name, asking about their family, and including them as we pray for our meal. A nice tip for their kind service and your unexpected kindness will bless both of you.

Blessing Your Server

Situated among gigantic trees and beautiful flower gardens is my favorite lunch spot, Cafe Batar. The cafe, located an hour north of Louisville, is like a breath of fresh air. The courteous and welcoming staff conveys, "Come in and enjoy."

They prepare their delicious entrée choices and scrumptious desserts on site. Homemade desserts and candies are available for purchase in the candy shop.

When seated, I spotted an interesting small card on our table. Surprised to see a name written across the middle of the card. It drew my attention. Now I could remember our server's name and bless them with a generous tip.

An Invitation to Church

Bob illustrates being generous with your server by inviting them to church. Then give them a generous tip. The next time you go to that restaurant, give them another generous tip—even a 50% tip. The third time, invite them to church again. Chances will be greater that their response is yes.

You want to guess what your server said to other workers concerning their day? I suspect they are talking a mile a minute regarding the people at one of their tables. Those folks who gave a very generous tip and prayed for them.

Please and Thank You

The hostess who greets you and takes you to your seat, those who fill your water glass and coffee cup, and even the manager, appreciate a polite please and thank you when they go beyond the call of duty. They will appreciate a nice generous tip.

We may never know the needs of those serving us unless we ask.

Sometimes things don't go well. Your steak isn't a good cut, or your food was not hot. Before complaining, consider what may have transpired in the kitchen. There may be more to the story. An incident may be beyond the chef's control.

I remember eating in a four-star restaurant where my steak was tough and difficult to chew. I pushed the meat aside and continued on with the rest of my dinner.

The server asked me, "Didn't you care for your steak?"

Now, what do I do? I tell the truth.

"I'm sorry, but it's tough, I can't chew it."

She was so embarrassed, "I will get you another steak."

And she did. The fresh one was tender and delicious.

Restaurants want the opportunity to correct your displeasure with a new order. Even the chef may not have a perfect evening. I can relate to that, can you? How many times have you as the "chef," messed up a meal? We need to forgive and forget.

The Biggest Tip Ever

A ministers' group was getting ready to pay for their dinner. One said to their server, "We are preachers and we thank you for your service to our table. Can we pray for you before we leave?"

The server relayed a story of needing money to pay his gas and electric bill. It was two months overdue and if he didn't pay $487.00 in the next couple of days, they would evict him from his apartment.

The ministers took pity on their server as he left to get their bill. One said, "Let's give him a big tip to help pay for that expense." So, they began gathering their money and when counted it was $147.00.

Then one in the group said, "Let's see if we can gather enough money to cover his entire $487.00 bill."

When they counted the money, they had $487.00!

A year later, one of those ministers went back to the restaurant. He asked the server, "What was the largest tip you know of someone receiving?"

"You won't believe this, but one server received $487.00. Could you pray for me too?"

Doesn't that warm your heart?

We may never know the needs of those serving us unless we ask.

People will hide their needs from others, unless they sense a genuineness from the person who asks how they are doing.

Attributes of kindness, grace, and generosity displayed to those outside our home and those who walk through our front doors are beautiful demonstrations of genuine hospitality.

CHAPTER 41

Party Ideas That are Simple and Fun

"Do not be foolish, but understand what the Lord's will is. Do not get drunk on wine, which leads to debauchery. Instead, be filled with the Spirit."

Ephesians 5:17, 18, NIV

PEOPLE LOVE PARTIES. But sometimes they are boring or guests cause trouble. Cut the wine and liquor, stop wild things, and plan clean fun activities.

I've shared with you several simple and detailed party ideas in earlier chapters. Here are a few more. And yes, I've done them all.

Candy Party

How about an old-fashioned candy store buffet? Let guests fill a small red box with candy at a Christmas party or a large gathering as dessert after dinner. Candy is a favorite and always good to serve with several choices.

Choose six or eight selections of candy, plus some nuts. Chocolate is a favorite of everyone and a must have. Add some hard candies, too. Cinnamon and lemon drops are big favorites. Supplies are easy to find online if needed. Check out the candy shop in your city or Oriental Trading Company online.

There are many ways to display candy for a party. Put candies in glass apothecary jars, adding stickers to the jars identifying each candy. Another way is to place a tent card in front of a jar. Offer tongs or scoops for getting a serving out. You only need six or eight selections of candy plus nuts.

Candy jars placed on a buffet, credenza or a long counter in your kitchen is a great way to serve assorted candy. Have cute little 4x3x3 inch boxes for people to hold their candy selections. Guests can fill the box and take candy home after the party.

If you decide against a box, use small plastic bowls and include tiny plastic bags for guests to take a few pieces home after the party.

Use self-serving water containers and put lemon or lime slices in the water. Use small throwaway cups and have a handy trash can available. Use colorful cocktail-sized napkins.

If you use a water dispenser often, invest in a good quality one. I've made the mistake more than once of having dispensers that are hard to use. Select one that the on/off spigot is easy to use and high enough off the counter that guests can put their glass or cup under it. You can rent dispensers too, avoiding any storage problems.

Enjoy a fun candy party.

Easter Egg Coloring Party

We decorate eggs with children. Why not our friends? What fun to ask a group of ladies to bring an old silk tie that belonged to their husband. Learn this silk tie decorating technique in Chapter 14. Wrap the egg in the tie and place in prepared water. Wait, and Voila! What a surprise when she unwraps the egg, as it may be a unique design, different from the tie.

Cookie Decorating Party

Easter or Christmas cookie decorating parties are fun to do. Yes, it takes time and effort to prepare, but worth doing. We've had these parties with college students, grandkids, friends, and staff groups. Everyone loves decorating cookies, especially when they know they can eat them later.

Pumpkin Carving Party

A great fall excursion is a hayride. Find a farm close by that sells pumpkins and does hayrides. Gather and carve pumpkins after the hayride. Have hotdogs to cook on a bonfire or just s'mores. And plenty of hot chocolate, as it could be a chilly evening.

Here's a tip: Since this event is not at your house, ask guests to bring their own pumpkin carving tools. Offer prizes for the best carving, worst carving, most creatively carved, and any other categories you can think of.

Slumber Party

Have you ever considered a slumber party for ladies? I did this with my choral group and pastors' wives a few times. Most of the ladies stayed awake all night. They bring their own sleeping bags and curl up in a corner or on a sofa. If lucky, they might get an actual bed. We eat and play games and tell stories. Try it. It will surprise you how much you will enjoy this childhood tradition.

Scavenger Hunts and Photo Shoots

Scavenger hunts are great for bonding a group together. List specific things guests are to find. If you are using phone cameras, list photos needed and announce the length of time to collect things. That's part of the challenge, beating the clock. Then head out in groups to seek and find.

Don't make it too easy, as you want them to be imaginative in their choices. Check out GooseChase.com[36] for adult scavenger hunt ideas.

Here is a sample of some things to find: an old log cabin, boat on a river, barking dog in someone's yard, swinging bridge, basketball goal, schoolhouse, and a church with a steeple. Or taking photos of your team in a car going through the car wash or climbing a tree. The list is endless for the ideas you can come up with.

Return to your house, show your photos, and share stories. Eat some snacks and announce the winners.

Your Next Party

Everyone loves a good party. Start planning your next fun gathering. Here are a few more ideas.

- Cookie Exchange
- Movie Night
- Scrapbooking Night
- Game Night
- White Elephant Exchange
- Luau Party
- Murder Mystery Night

CHAPTER 42

Ideas for Quick Dinner Parties

"He rained down manna for the people to eat,
he gave them the grain of heaven."

Psalm 78:24, NIV

NEED IDEAS FOR dinner parties that are lots of fun but not so laborious that you don't enjoy the party too?

These party ideas are ones we have done in our home. Spending time and having dinner with friends are some of the greatest times you will ever have. I hope some of these casual dinner party ideas will spur you to pick up your phone and text some couples to come for dinner and an evening of elbows on your table.

Enjoy this time together as you share prayer requests and encourage one another. Everyone needs encouragement. There can't be a better place to do that than in your home.

An Old-Fashioned Pitch In

Often, we've invited folks to come and share in the cooking and preparation. Make a list of ingredients and text it to your guests. My Snow on the Mountain recipe is a great dish for this kind of evening with friends.

Your guests could also select what they will fix ahead of time and bring to your house. People enjoy helping. Some call it the Grub Club and each couple brings a dish. The host prepares the meat. It can be as simple as hot dogs, baked beans, and potato salad. Or as elaborate as steaks on the grill, baked potatoes, and a salad.

Baked Potato Bar

Invite friends to bring assorted potato toppings. Prepare the potatoes ahead of time and keep them warm until serving time.[37] Make sure they are fully cooked and soft when you squeeze them. There is nothing worse than a hard baked potato for the main course. Just before serving, slice the potatoes lengthwise about halfway through and push at the ends.

Here is a list from *beautyandbedlam.com*[38] for the ultimate baked potato bar.

- Large Idaho Potatoes
- Salt and Pepper
- Butter and Sour Cream
- Shredded Cheese
- Chili
- Bacon Bits or Crumbled Bacon
- Finely Chopped Green Onions
- Sauteed Red or Vidalia Onions and Peppers
- Steamed Broccoli
- Diced Tomatoes
- Warmed Nacho Cheese Sauce
- Guacamole
- Jalapeno Peppers
- Olives
- Herbs
- Diced Chicken, Barbecue Chicken, Steak, Ham, Pork, Taco Meat

Waffle Bar

Prepare the waffles from a favorite mix or recipe. To keep them crisp after cooking, lay them on a wire rack on a cookie sheet uncovered and put them in a 200-degree oven until you are ready to serve them.

Ask friends to bring assorted syrup flavors, chocolate chips, nuts, berries, bananas, cinnamon apples, roasted pears, grilled pineapple, and whipped cream. To complement the waffles, serve slices of ham, bacon, sausage, or fried chicken.

Christmas Soup Buffet

It is fun during the holidays to invite friends or family for dinner to enjoy a soup buffet. If it's family, they can help decorate your Christmas tree. Invite your Sunday school class, small group, or Bible study group to come together in a different, more casual setting.

The guests bring their favorite soup to share for dinner. The hostess will have plastic bowls, plates, spoons, napkins, and drinks. Others in the group can bring cookies and brownies.

Plan a needed fundraiser, a speaker, or entertainment by someone to top off the evening. Or encourage folks to bring a favorite game. Casual evenings sometimes turn out to be the most inspirational.

Chili Soup Night

Guests savor bowls of chili, cheese, and crackers. This is a superb evening meal before watching a football or basketball game.

Men's Chili Cook-Off

People bring pots of chili prepared at home. Judges will do a taste test to see which chili recipe is the best. They award prizes for first, second, and third place. A sleeve of golf balls or a gift card is a good prize. Have ribbons available for first, second, and third place. Serve assorted cheese and crackers along with the varieties of chili.

Pie or Cake Bake Off

Ladies bring their favorite pies, someone judges, and prizes are given. A plant or bouquet or gift cards for awards are nice. Nothing elaborate. A men's bake-off is always a good time, too.

A Summer Cookout

Grilling hamburgers and hotdogs on the outdoor grill makes a great summer yard party. Serve baked beans, potato salad, sliced watermelon, fresh sliced tomatoes, corn on the cob, and chips. Have cookies for dessert or ice cream with summer fruits such as berries or peaches. Why not try your hand at homemade ice cream?

Charcuterie Boards

Need a quick and fun idea for gathering with family and friends? How about a charcuterie board? The ideas and themes to artfully arrange one are endless.

Choose a variety of cheeses, meats, fresh and dried fruits, vegetables, artisan breads, crackers, nuts, cookies, jams, and sauces that complement each other. Several items for tasty boards and grazing together may already be on your pantry shelves and in the refrigerator.

You say, I'm not artistic. Balance and quality food items are key to a successful presentation. Start with larger items such as meats and cheeses, and then add bread and crackers. Next, place fruits and greens to garnish the board and fill in the spaces.

Instead of doing boards by yourself, include family or friends to decorate and prepare a board together. Couples can bring assorted cheeses and fruits to the party. Give them a food list from which to choose specific items to bring.

There are numerous books and articles found online with a gazillion ideas for sizes and shapes of boards, recipes, portion amounts per person, and many more helpful tips. If you don't have a wooden board, pull out your cookie sheets and platters. Even parchment paper can be spread out on the counter or table.

Check online for many places to order a completed board—designed and prepared with packaged food items—that will be shipped to your home.

Charcuterie boards are great conversation starters as guests gather around the table choosing food to nibble and eat. Your group will love this time. A plus for the hostess is that the preparation is done ahead of time and the board is self-serve. You can enjoy talking with your guests as you graze together.

CHAPTER 43

University of Kentucky Fundraiser

"Now to him who is able to do immeasurably more than
all we ask or imagine, according to his power that is at work
within us, to him be glory in the church and in Christ Jesus
throughout all generations, forever and ever! Amen.**"**

Ephesians 3:20, 21, NIV

THE LEAVES WERE turning orange, red, and gold. Folks started
decorating their porches with colorful chrysanthemums along
with orange and white pumpkins. I love this time of the year,
and it's my favorite time to entertain groups. In my wildest
dreams, I never expected to host this worthy cause. But God
knows best!

One morning, Bob began telling me about the interesting phone call he just received.

The University of Kentucky athletic director called him, asking if we could help raise money for the Christian Student Fellowship's new building. The CSF students needed a larger building. The athletic director explained that the students held their weekly devotional meetings and Bible studies in a small, compact building. The CSF ministry hosts a luau for over 5,000 students during the first week of school. On Friday nights they host a pancake dinner for students.

Other times they host non-alcoholic parties in the same building. This was a tough task—trying to cram 800-1000 students into a space only big enough for half that many people. Many students would spill out onto the sidewalk and street during the wintry weather.

Bob finished telling me about the phone call and then he said, "I told the athletic director, 'yes.'"

Questioning him, "Where and when will it be?"

Pointing to the floor, he said, "Here. Someone from the CSF office will call you."

I'm thinking, 'here? At our house?'

It stunned me! Our entire family has been die-hard University of Louisville sports fans for over 50 years, not UK fans. UK is our biggest rival.

But never mind favorite teams now. This event was for college students desperate to meet together, studying Scripture and the life of Jesus. Count me in on doing this event!

The next day, I received a call from a CSF staff member. We discovered only a few evenings were available. A dessert for a sizeable group on such brief notice will work best.

I thought, they will most likely schedule it for an evening in November. Plenty of time to gather names of friends who were UK fans and plan the evening.

Instead, I got a text asking if we might host an event in ten days. Ten days? Is this the only date the athletic director and Christian Student Fellowship director are available? The two directors both needed to be here.

I swallowed hard and said, "Well, I need to check with Bob. It's our grandson's football game. Even though he may not play, we still want to cheer for the team."

Bob and I discussed the date and decided we needed to say yes. We hurried to collect names, addresses, and emails of friends who were UK fans and sent invitations out eight days before the evening. It wasn't ideal to host an event on Friday night and send invitations arriving less than a week prior. We shall see.

I ordered an assortment of individual cakes from the "Nothing Bundt Cake" shop. They packaged each cake in a transparent plastic box. Guests could eat it at the party or take it home and save it for later. We served hot apple cider and coffee—perfect for the chilly fall evening.

I wanted to use UK blue colors and had blue forks and napkins. It was harder than I thought to find those colors in plastic ware. Ah, but royal blue will look nice with fall colors.

I read you should have blue in every bouquet of mixed flowers. So orange pumpkins and mums and a hint of blue would be perfect.

While shopping, I spotted a weathered wooden lantern. Attached to the top was a stem with large blue flowers and assorted blue ribbons made into a bow.

Hm, I've been considering adding navy or royal blue to the color scheme in my dining room. This will work!

Blue napkins, plastic cups, and forks purchased, cakes ordered, and cider in the refrigerator—ready and perfect for the end of October. And no plates, silverware, or cups to wash. It was easy cleanup. Just throw it away. Now, I was getting excited.

I didn't have a hot drink dispenser anymore and bought a new one. I ordered it online to arrive a couple days before the event. That was enough time to see if it worked.

The night of the fundraiser, I poured the cider into the dispenser. Yay, everything was still working.

People began arriving, and several were standing around the kitchen island.

Hot cider began spewing out the back of the dispenser. Our church's college minister was the alumnus giving a CSF testimony. He grabbed towels and started sopping up the cider. I reached around the dispenser to pull up the lid. Stupid me! The steam pouring out was burning my fingers.

I grabbed an ice cube, pressed it on my fingers, and wrapped a paper towel tight around them. I needed to stop the burning and stinging pain. I soon discovered the ice and pressure stopped the pain, and no blisters developed.

People didn't realize I burned my fingers. CSF staff helped me serve. Those young people were a blessing.

I enjoy doing something unexpected for our guests. My idea for this group was a small orange rubber basketball you squeeze in your hand as a party favor. We wrote with permanent magic marker CSF on the balls, giving one to every guest as a reminder to pray for CSF and their needs.

Bob surprised our guests by having two former UK basketball players attend. We celebrated one of the former player's birthdays, surprising him with a cake and singing "Happy Birthday." Just a simple little extra touch for guests.

The athletic director and CSF directors spoke giving information on CSF. A current student and an alumnus shared inspiring testimonies of how their lives changed when they surrendered to Christ.

The evening was a tremendous success. I am glad we said yes when asked to host this fundraiser in our home. It far exceeded our expectations. Thirty guests committed over one million dollars. I cried when the University of Kentucky group told us. There were more funds coming to help fund the Christian Student Fellowship's new building project. Why do we underestimate the power of God?

Afterword

"Offer hospitality to one another without grumbling. Each of
you should use whatever gift you have received to serve others,
as faithful stewards of God's grace in its various forms."

(1 Peter 4:9,10, NIV)

Judy has numerous, God-given talents. The gifts of music, ad-
ministration, prayer, discernment, and serving all come natu-
rally to her. Initially, the gift of hospitality was not my wife's
strongest gift. However, over the years she "practiced hospitality" (Romans 12:13 NIV), and over time she became an expert
at it. She had little option—she was married to me!

When I was growing up, my mother entertained sponta-
neous dinner guests almost every Sunday and to this day, I very
much enjoy having guests in our home. After all, it's a biblical
command to "Offer hospitality to one another without grumbling"! (1 Peter 4:9 NIV)

In the early years of our marriage two things made practicing hospitality challenging for Judy. First, she is by nature, a
perfectionist. Her perfectionistic tendencies are a tremendous
advantage to me (most of the time) but when we were preparing
for guests, it made her tense. Like Jesus' friend Martha, she was
"worried and upset about many things."

The second thing that made hospitality difficult was me.
As she mentions in this book, I brought home some guests who

were challenging and sometimes I didn't give enough advance notice. Occasionally I gave no advance notice at all; they just showed up!

I erroneously assumed practicing hospitality was easy. It's not. I've matured a little over the years and have become a little more helpful around the house. But early on, I took it for granted there would be extra food in the refrigerator and clean sheets on the guest bed.

Over the years, Judy practiced hospitality—and she almost always did it without grumbling. She became really good at entertaining and very comfortable with it. Today when guests are present, she enjoys them and enjoys herself. Since she's more relaxed, those gracing our table are soon comfortable enough to put their elbows on the table and feel right at home.

We've had some hilarious and edifying experiences in our house because Judy was willing to welcome guests and serve them. Our two boys and our seven grandchildren have had exposure to spiritual giants visiting us and those saints have impacted them forever.

The lifelong friendships we've developed and the spiritual memories we've created by entertaining guests have helped mature our entire family.

I pray the experiences and suggestions Judy has included in this book will motivate many to open their homes and, "Offer hospitality to one another without grumbling." Your lives and the lives of your children will be greatly enriched.

And who knows? Maybe you'll be the recipient of the promise in (Hebrews 13:2 NIV), "Do not forget to show hospitality to strangers, for by so doing some people have shown hospitality to angels without knowing it."

—Bob Russell

Recipes

Tuna Casserole

Ingredients:
2 ½ cups of small egg noodles
Scant teaspoon butter or oil
Water
2 large cans of chunk light tuna in water
1 can cream of mushroom soup
¼ cup milk
2 cups shredded cheddar cheese
Salt and pepper

1. Cook noodles in large sauce pan filled with water and drain.
2. Stir in teaspoon of butter or oil so noodles do not stick together.
3. Add dash of salt.
4. In casserole dish, add the drained tuna and mushroom soup.
5. Pour milk in soup can and swish around.
6. Add to tuna and soup mixture.
7. Add the cheese, dash or two of salt and pepper and the cooked noodles.
8. Stir all ingredients together.
9. Bake at 350 degrees for 20-30 minutes until bubbly. This could also be cooked in the microwave.
10. Serves 4-6

Snow on the Mountain

This Polynesian recipe will serve 12 people.

Ingredients:
8 cups cooked, cut up chicken. About 4-6 large chicken breasts. (Ask butcher to cut up in small ½ inch cubes.)
4 cups chicken broth (I use a good quality boxed chicken broth rather than broth from cooking the chicken, it is richer tasting.)
9 Tablespoons butter
4 cups of half and half
1½ teaspoon salt
½ teaspoon pepper
1 pound of fresh mushrooms sliced. (I buy cooked mushroom pieces in a jar.)
1 cup flour

Cook chicken and set aside.

1. In a large heavy pan, melt butter and add flour and broth. Use a whisk and whisk rapidly as you gradually mix flour in the mixture. I have discovered pouring broth and flour in a little at a time is best. You do not want it to curdle.
2. Cook until boiling and thick, stirring every few minutes, so it does not stick.
3. Add half and half, stirring as you add to the sauce. Do not boil. Cook until heated through.
4. Add cooked chicken, mushrooms, salt and pepper.

Place ingredients for mountain in bowls and set on the counter in order given.

1. 10 cups of cooked rice
2. Creamed chicken with sliced mushrooms. Serve from pan cooked in to keep hot, or place in a large soup tureen.

3. 4 to 6 medium tomatoes, sliced or chopped into chunks, your preference
4. 3 to 4 very small bunches of green onions, about 1 cup, sliced and chopped
5. 2 cans of Chow Mein noodles
6. 8 stalks of chopped celery. If in a hurry, I go to a salad station at the grocery store and get the chopped celery prepared for salads.
7. 2 jars of sliced/chopped, stuffed olives. I buy the salad olives already cut up.
8. ¾ lb. shredded Colby or Longhorn cheese. Buy the 16-ounce package of the shredded cheese.
9. 2 #2 cans of crushed pineapple in water, drained
10. 3 3-ounce packages of blanched, unsalted slivered or sliced almonds
11. 2 small packages or cans of shredded coconut for the "snow" on the mountain. I prefer the cans as the coconut is moister.

Invite guests to spoon the rice onto the middle of their plates. Then ladle the chicken sauce over the rice. Add other foods on the mountain in the order listed. And the final touch will be a surprise to everyone gathered. Sprinkle the moist, white shredded coconut on top of the mountain. Thus, Snow on the Mountain! It is delicious and fun. You will love serving this recipe to friends and family.

Accompaniment foods could be a frozen salad or pear salad. Serve warm bread and lots of softened butter.

I sometimes double the recipe and save half of the sauce for leftovers. You can put it in freezer bags for a winter's day. It makes great soup. If needed, add one or two cans of chicken in water to the sauce. Add boxed chicken stock from the grocery store if you want it to be a thinner soup. This is also the perfect comfort food for a winter evening.

Snow on the Mountain makes a wonderful dinner for a large group. You can double the recipe and have guests bring the toppings. The host does the chicken sauce and rice.

Cranberry Banana Frozen Salad

1 8-ounce package of cream cheese
1 Tablespoon mayonnaise
2 Tablespoon white sugar
1 cup pineapple, crushed
1 large banana, sliced and diced or chopped
½ cup chopped nuts, pecans, or walnuts. (Add more if desired.)
1 can cranberry sauce, or whole berry sauce
1 package of Dream Whip

Mix and beat together the cream mixture of mayonnaise and sugar until creamy. Add pineapple, banana, nuts, and cranberry sauce. Whip envelope of Dream Whip and fold into ingredients. Freeze in bread pan and slice or put in molds. Freeze overnight. Double recipe and put in a 9x13 pan. Cut in squares and place on lettuce leaf.

Pear Dressing for Salad Greens

Bottle of White Balsamic Vinaigrette (Vinaigrette is found in the refrigerated salad dressing section.)
2 cans unsweetened sliced pears in natural juice.

1. Pour vinaigrette into blender.
2. Add 1 can pear juice into the blender, reserving the pears.
3. Add second can of pears and juice to blender with the vinaigrette and blend until creamy.

1. Place Organic Spring Salad greens on individual salad plates and lay the reserved sliced pears on top.
2. Sprinkle with walnuts and Feta Cheese.
3. Pour dressing on top when ready to place on table.

Banana Crème Brulee

Ingredients:
2 quarts whipping cream
2 tsp of high-quality Pure Vanilla Extract
16 egg yokes
1 cup sugar
2/3 cup brown sugar, packed
Ripe bananas

1. Combine all ingredients and mix well. Pour in ramekins or ceramic baking dish and place in hot water bath in a 350 degrees oven. Bake until firm. It takes approximately 1½ hours to bake.
2. Then chill several hours.
3. Top each ramekin with one sliced banana arranged neatly in a pan.
4. Dust the top with raw or granulated sugar evenly, approximately 1/16" to 1/8".
5. Brown the sugar under the broiler or with a propane torch.
6. Baking time has varied for me depending on how much of the recipe I prepare. I usually divide it.
7. Instead of using bananas, try a few assorted berries sprinkled on top after caramelized.

Nana's Chocolate Chip Cookies

¾ cup white sugar
¾ cup brown sugar, packed
1 cup buttery shortening (Crisco) or two sticks of butter
1 teaspoon vanilla extract dripping over the side of spoon
2 eggs

Blend above ingredients together in a mixer until creamy.

Add:
¼ teaspoon salt
½ teaspoon soda
2¼ cups of flour (Do not sift the flour.)
1 16-ounce package of chocolate chips. (Preferably Hershey's, they are a little richer tasting.)

Mix all the ingredients into the cream mixture until blended.
Drop by teaspoon or small scoop onto a non-greased cookie sheet.

Bake at 375 degrees for about 10-15 minutes, depending on whether you want them crisp or soft.

Mother's Devils Food Chocolate Cake

½ cup of cocoa
1½ cup of flour
1½ cup of sugar
1¼ tsp of soda
½ tsp of salt
½ cup shortening
1 cup sour milk*
1 tsp vanilla
2 large eggs

*My mother used to keep a small jar of sour milk in the refrigerator, but if she didn't have enough, she used this method: warm milk in microwave. Add 1Tablespoon vinegar to the 1 cup of milk. Stir, let it stand a few minutes and it is ready for the recipe. Tastes terrible in the cup, but great in recipe.

1. Stir dry ingredients.
2. Add shortening, milk and vanilla.
3. Mix together and beat 2 minutes.
4. Then add eggs and beat 2 more minutes.
5. Pour into two greased and floured, 9" baking pans or one 9" x 13" pan.
6. Bake at 350 degrees for 25-30 minutes.
7. Stick a tooth pick in center of cakes to test if completely baked.
8. When fully baked, remove from oven and place on a cooling rack.
9. Ice with favorite chocolate icing after cake has cooled.

Turkey Chili

2-3 pounds lean ground turkey
2 Tbs olive oil
½ cup celery, chopped
½ cup onion, chopped
½ cup green pepper, chopped
2 Tbs roasted garlic
2 cans mild chili beans
2 cans tomatoes with green chilies
2 cans tomato sauce
2 envelopes low sodium and mild chili seasoning
Spaghetti for bowls of soup
Assorted grated cheeses for garnish

1. Cook ground turkey in separate pan. I parboil the meat until crumbly and no pink. Drain and set aside.
2. In separate pan, pour olive oil and warm.
3. Add vegetable mixture and garlic. Cook, until vegetables are translucent and stir so vegetables will not stick.
4. Add ground turkey meat to vegetable mixture.
5. Add chili beans, tomatoes with green chilies, and tomato sauce.
6. Pour water in cans to rinse out, and add that water to soup mixture.
7. Add chili seasoning.
8. Cook until bubbly and turn down to simmer.

The soup can be served immediately or simmer for several hours. Keep watching closely and add water if necessary.

At serving time, add a little spaghetti to individual bowls. Make assorted grated cheeses available for top of soup. Or have cheese slices available with crackers for a side.

A serving dish of bread and butter pickles and a plate of celery and carrot sticks are great as additional side items.

Set out a jar of peanut butter for crackers. Our family likes peanut butter on crackers when having chili. Try it and enjoy.

Tuna Sandwiches

1 small can of tuna in water
¼ cup of walnut pieces
1 crisp apple
3 Heaping tablespoons of mayonnaise

1. Drain tuna from water in can.
2. Add walnuts.
3. Slice half of apple and chop into small pieces, adding to tuna mixture.
4. Slice other half of apple and lay pieces on two plates.
5. Add mayonnaise.
6. Stir ingredients until covered with mayonnaise.
7. Scoop the tuna salad onto toasted heavy grain bread slices to make a sandwich. Slice from corner to corner.
8. Or, you can take a juicy tomato and cut it in quarters. Lay pieces out on the plate. Scoop tuna salad on the tomato.
9. Add chips and grapes or apples to the plate.
10. Makes two sandwiches.

Grilled Cheese Sandwich

Two slices of heavy grain bread
Butter
3 slices of cheese, such as Havarti cheese, cheddar cheese, Swiss cheese or Pepper Jack cheese
Mayhaw jelly or a jelly or jam of your choice that would go with cheese

1. Butter one side of each slice of bread.
2. Layer the three cheese slices. Spoon the jelly between two of the slices of cheese.
3. Place slices together, butter side out and place on an electric panini press or on a cookie sheet and under the broiler of your oven.
4. Carefully watch if in oven. Let bread brown and cheese start to melt. Turn over once. A panini press is easier because there is no turning over.
5. Add cooked bacon or tomato. Do your own thing to make your grilled cheese delicious.

Baked Potatoes

Baking Potatoes
Olive Oil
Garlic
Salt

1. Preheat the oven to 375 degrees.
2. Scrub the potatoes well and dry.
3. Rub the potato skins with olive oil and or garlic over the skin.
4. Sprinkle with salt.
5. Poke a few tiny holes in the potato with a fork.
6. Wrap in foil for baking in oven.
7. Bake for 1 hour.
8. If you want to cook the potatoes quicker, wrap in aluminum foil and parboil them in a large pan on top of the stove. When finished cooking, pull them from the water and place on a wire rack over the sink, and wipe the foil dry with a towel.

Recipes for a Crowd

Pork Cutlets or Cubed Steak

Ingredients for 50

50 Pork cutlets or cubed steak
Salt and pepper
Flour for dredging meat
Cooking oil
3 22.6-ounce cans of cream of mushroom soup

1. Sprinkle salt and pepper on meat.
2. Dredge each piece of meat in a shallow pan of flour.
3. Brown in a large oiled skillet until crispy.
4. Begin layering in large steam table pans.
5. Pour the cream of mushroom soup between each layer.
6. Cover pans with aluminum foil.
7. Bake at 200 degrees for 3 to 4 hours.

If you want to use this for your family of four or five, it's easy to do. Buy cutlets or steaks and brown. Pour one or two number #2 sized cans of cream of mushroom soup over the meat and cook in the oven at 200 degrees all afternoon.

Lasagna

Ingredients for 50

20 pounds of extra lean ground beef
Salt and pepper
Italian seasonings jar
Roasted garlic
2 32-ounce jars of Italian spaghetti sauce or Marinara sauce per two pounds of meat.
2 enormous bags of shredded mozzarella cheese
2 large cartons of ricotta cheese
32 ounces of cottage cheese
1 cup of parmesan cheese
½ cup water
4 eggs
2 enormous boxes of lasagna noodles

1. Prepare meat sauce, by parboiling in water. Cover meat with the water.
2. Cook through until meat is crumbly. Strain in a colander.
3. Return meat to pan and add spaghetti or Marinara sauce.
4. Stir until mixed and hot.
5. If needed, season with salt and pepper and Italian seasonings.
6. Mix cheeses, eggs, and water.

7. Spoon light layer of meat sauce in bottom of steam table pan.
8. Layer with uncooked noodles, spoon the meat sauce along with the cheese and egg mixture between layers of noodles, filling the pan.
9. Cover with foil and place in the oven.
10. Cook in 200-250 degrees oven all afternoon.
11. Ovens vary, so be observant for the first few times.

Endnotes

1   Find the tuna casserole recipe in the Appendix.
2   Find more information and a form to apply at https://www.bobrussell.org/mentoring-ministers/
3   Nabeel Qureshi, *Seeking Allah, Finding Jesus: A Devout Muslim Encounters Christianity* (Zondervan, 2016).
4   Nabeel Qureshi, *No God but One: Allah or Jesus?: A Former Muslim Investigates the Evidence for Islam and Christianity* (Zondervan, 2016).
5   Pastry Chef Online, www.pastrychefonline.com/bread-butter-and-sugar-sandwich.
6   Porch Sitter's Union, https://porchsittersunion.com/about-us-porch-sitting/
7   Kristen Schell, *The Turquoise Table* (Nashville: Thomas Nelson, 2017).
8   N.T. Wright, *The Day the Revolution Began: Reconsidering the Meaning of Jesus's Crucifixion* (HarperOne, 2016).
9   https://voice.dts.edu/article/a-place-at-the-table-jones-barry/
10 Find the Snow on the Mountain recipe in the Appendix.
11 Chip Ingram, *The Genius of Generosity*, (National Christian Foundation, 2010).
12 Becky Hand, "The Benefits of Eating Together", https://www.sparkpeople.com/resource/ nutrition_articles.asp?id=439
13 Leonard Sweet, *Tablet to Table* (NavPress 2014)
14 Tom Kersting, *Disconnected (Baker Books 2020)*
15 Nancy Gibbs, "The Magic of the Family Meal", 2005, https://www.organicconsumers.org/news/magic-family-meal
16 Find the chocolate cake recipe in the Appendix.

17 Henri Nouwen, https://henrinouwen.org/meditation/the-mea
l-that-makes-us-family-and-friends/

18 Find the tuna sandwich and grilled cheese sandwich recipes in the
Appendix.

19 Shauna Niequist, *Bread and Wine* (Zondervan, 2013).

20 Annie Falk, *Palm Beach Entertaining* (Random House Inc, 2012).

21 Kelley Nan https://kelleynan.com/

22 Sandy Coughlin, "Teaching Our Families About Setting the
Table", 2005, *The Reluctant Entertainer*, https://reluctantenter-
tainer.com/teaching-our-families-about-setting-the-table/.

23 "Friends" by Michael W. Smith and Debbie Smith.

24 "Friends" by Michael W. Smith and Debbie Smith.

25 "Friends" by Michael W. Smith and Debbie Smith.

26 Florence Littauer, *Silver Boxes: The Gift of Encouragement*
(Thomas Nelson, 1989).

27 Rebecca Manley Pippert, *Spirituality According to Jesus*
(Saltshaker Resources, 2004).

28 Liz Curtis Higgs, *The Women of Easter* (Crown Publishing
Group, 2017).

29 Warren Wiersbe, *Be Rich* (Scripture Press, 1986).

30 Nancy Sleeth, *Almost Amish: One Woman's Quest for a Slower,
Simpler, More Sustainable Life* (Tyndale House: 2012).

31 https://www.faithward.org/diy-resurrection-eggs-for-holy-week/

32 Kenneth Taylor, *The Bible in Pictures for Little Eyes* (Moody
Press 1956),

33 Gloria Gaither and Shirley Dobson, *Let's Make a Memory* (Word
Publishing 1994).

34 Annie Falk, *Palm Beach Entertaining* (Random House Inc, 2012).

35 https://togetherkit.com/icebreakers-for-adults-questions.html

36 GooseChase, https://www.goosechase.com/

37 Find a recipe for preparing baked potatoes in the Appendix.

38 Jen Schmidt, *Balancing Beauty and Bedlam*, https://beautyand-
bedlam.com/

Countless Thanks

Stopped at a traffic light, my phone lights up bright. It's Ruth.

"Hello, my friend. You will write a book and I will help you."

Stammering as I begin speaking, "I can't write a book. We are moving in a couple of weeks. Holidays are fast approaching, and we go to Florida for two months after Christmas. Besides, what do I have to say?"

Her gentle reply, "I want you to write about being a pastor's wife and how you entertain and show hospitality." As she expanded on her idea, I listened.

"Ruth, thank you, but I need to discuss this with Bob and my family."

Five months later, I started thinking about this book.

So, Ruth Schenk, thank you for pushing me to do this project and encouraging me when I wasn't sure I could. I appreciate all your help, encouragement, and getting me started.

Thanks to my family and close friends who encouraged me and waited for this book. Thank you to Facebook friends and church friends from Southeast and around the world. My prayer is you enjoy the stories and tips and goof ups. Some of you may spot yourselves, and say "I was there." "I remember!"

Thank you, Patt Senseman and Sharon Lowen, for reading, correcting, and extending encouraging words from the beginning.

To the Butter Babes, who prayed and encouraged me through my labors of pulling all these stories together. The four of you—Elizabeth, Bonnie, Nancy, and Fay—listened as I read stories at many lunches, and you each read many others. Thank you for your encouragement and ideas.

Along with Pat H., Nancy S., Liz H., my Bible study table group, Laurie B., Susan T., Val M., Gigi G., Angela C., and countless others who read some of those first story drafts, encouraging me along the way. Thank you, each one.

Thank you, Patt Senseman, for taking me to the end of this project. For pulling everything together during some hectic months in my life and forging on to get the finished product to the publisher.

Thank you, Karis Pratt, for the design, making it special, and then completing the cover project.

To my longtime friend, Martha Brammer, thank you for your time given to do the sketches throughout the book.

Thank you to Nick Bonura, our photographer, for coming to my rescue and doing what I needed in a short time.

To my husband Bob, thank you for spending many mornings reading over my chapters, leaving comments, and cheering me on to completion.

Thank you to each of the endorsers for giving your valuable time to read *Elbows on the Table*.

This project would never have reached completion without each of you. I sincerely thank you.

Family Photos

Russell Family

Charlie Russell Family

Our Children's Memories

"When I think about my mom and hospitality, I remember our first house in a Louisville middle-class neighborhood. The kitchen was tiny, the furnishings and appliances were modest.

My dad frequently invited people to come over for fellowship, usually after Sunday night church or a weeknight softball game. Almost always the invitation came with a promise: "Judy will make chocolate chip cookies!" That was all it took for a gathering-the promise of Judy's cookies. I remember the laughter filling the house as the adults crammed around our kitchen table and little children played in the family room not far away.

When a teenager, my friends would sometimes ask, "If we come over, will your mom bake cookies?" We crammed around the kitchen table just like my parents and their friends had done for years. Nobody cared that my house wasn't the nicest in town. Cookies in the kitchen provided the perfect environment for great memories. I have lifelong friendships that were forged around that kitchen table.

The Bible commands us to offer hospitality for our own benefit and the benefit of others. I hope my mom's book inspires people to reconsider ways they can open their home to friends, family, and those in need. My mom encouraged us. May we reclaim the lost art of hospitality."
— Rusty

"There are many lessons I have learned from Judy. Whether she is being a gracious hostess to a large dinner party of influential guests or a small gathering of close friends and family, she is fully committed to organization and proper etiquette.

There is always design and coordination to the table settings, even if we are using paper plates and plastic cups. No matter the occasion, she incorporates a theme and a pleasant atmosphere.

At first glance, this insistence on good manners and fancy tables may seem superficial or fussy. However, in a family where the men far outnumber the women, Judy has modeled her own classic feminine beauty. It would have been far too easy to just let it go and let the busyness of life and ministry and the love of watching sports from the sofa dictate a culture of casualness in her home. But that would not have been true to who she is.

She has inspired all of us to appreciate those gatherings around her table. They are characterized by intentionality, and we are free to enjoy each other and cherish the memories that are made there."

— Kellie

"When I was about seven or eight years old, our church was growing rapidly, and my mom anticipated there might be times church members would invite our family to fancy dinners. She was understandably concerned my brother and I lacked the manners and etiquette to conduct ourselves during such occasions. One evening she planned a formal dinner in our dining room for our family as "practice."

It may come as a surprise, but I was not the most compliant child. If the dinner didn't include pizza or something with peanut butter or some chocolate chip cookies, I was not interested, and I certainly didn't care about where my elbows were or placing one hand on my lap or which side of the plate to place my fork. My brother benefited from the fact that I was not bashful about making any of that known, and he also bristled.

Eventually, my mom abandoned her plan to enforce the rules of etiquette and instead warned us that we might embarrass ourselves if we didn't attempt to learn proper social skills. Of course, her warning was prophetic. A few years later, Dad was a guest speaker at a formal banquet, and I inadvertently flipped my salad plate onto a stranger seated next to me.

One of the things I love about my mom is while she strives to make moments elegant and lovely, she does not make them uncomfortable or stuffy. If you are blessed to sit around a table prepared by my mom, you might find it set with fancy china, but you will also find an abundance of laughter and joy. And you will most certainly find room for your elbows."

— Phil

"I don't have a lot of memories where Judy messed things up or forgot something because that isn't Judy. Judy is a fastidious housekeeper. She is very detail-oriented and appreciates things being in their place.

Having said that I will say that she has shown an immense amount of grace and mercy to me (and Phil) over the past 30 years of doing life with them.

Our family has grown from the two of us to now having three almost grown children.

We've celebrated almost every holiday and birthday at their house because her house is always "ready for guests." This makes things much easier for me because I'm not ever ready for guests!

When our daughter Corrie turned six, I wanted to do a fancy tea party for her birthday party. When I asked Judy if we could use her dining room, she got excited and offered some ideas to help host it. She even went to the trouble of offering some of her hats, scarves, gloves, and mirrors so the girls could have an impromptu dress up activity. Seven little girls in the dining room for tea, little sandwiches, and cake was a sweet memory."

— Lisa

Friends Memories

"From the beautiful seasonal wreaths on her front door to the flowers on the tables, Judy's home is alive with color and pizzazz. These are only trumped by her graciousness to anyone who drops by. When I am a guest there, I notice she carefully attends to each small detail which has been placed in just the right spot so that her home says, "I am happy you are here," "Please feel comfortable, enjoy yourself," and "I care about you."
—Susan

"My fondest memory of being in Judy's home was years ago when I first came to Louisville and her boys were little. We sat on lawn chairs in the family room, as many young couples do. Of course. sometimes we had the famous chocolate chip cookies but so many times it was as simple as popcorn. Everyone likes popcorn! It was simple, it was good, it gave a warm old-fashioned feeling and we didn't feel like we had caused a lot of trouble. Just sweet fun was to be had. Sometimes the simplest of hospitality is the most memorable. We loved it!"
–Marty

"I'll always remember the first time I went to Judy's home. On the front porch on a chalk board, in her personal handwriting was the word "Welcome". So fitting, it made me feel the warmth and love. Judy's hospitality is all about her guests and making each one special. Judy loves dinner table conversations. They are very special to her. They are spiritual, meaningful and fun but never frivolous."

–Georgia

"Judy is generous and creative. She does everything with excellence, exceeds all expectations, and makes hospitality look so easy. The ambience is always great, soothing and relaxing. I can recount times when I have stayed in her home and been stressed from issues in my life. She has a calming effect on me. She is relaxing and peaceful. That is hospitality coming from her heart with the desire to honor the Lord.

Judy helps her friends feel special when they celebrate their birthday. I recall a time when she asked each lady in our small group to write something about ourselves, including colors we liked, and hobbies and other personal interest stories. She then had an artistic friend make each of us gorgeous cards that depicted our individual personality. What a gift and a treasure it made for each of us, and we all felt so special when our birthday arrived.

When hospitality comes from one's heart, it is genuine."

–Jane

"When I recall the number of preachers that have sat at Judy's table, I have this vision of the celebration and gathering she and Bob will enjoy in heaven someday. So many friends from over the years that they have encouraged in their faith journey, all together, worshiping the Lord and enjoying fellowship together."

–Sherry

Great is Thy Faithfulness

A special thanks to my grandson, Charlie Russell, the original cover designer for *Elbows on the Table*. He could not complete what he envisioned to be the finished product, because of COVID-19.

Charlie sent a text. "Nana, it's a good thing we canceled the photo shoot this weekend. I have COVID!"

Within a week, Charlie was in the ICU with COVID-19 Pneumonia. Visitors forbidden to visit and doctors and nurses masked.

Four days later, he watched the birth of his first child through Facetime, two floors away. Charity Rose entered this crazy world.

Then, an unexpected text. "Charlie is being intubated!" We wept tears of anxiety and dread. As his oxygen level dropped to 70, his heart raced, fever spiked, and medicines didn't work. Doctors scrambled to keep him alive with machines, medicines, and constant bedside care.

They told us his chances would be better if an ECMO machine could be found; but none were available. Thankfully, God heard our cry, and the next day one was secured. Charlie was air-lifted to the Nashville hospital where his wife worked.

Our nerves teetered on edge, with sleepless nights and stressful days. Charlie, heavily sedated, slept; while ECMO, dialysis, ventilator, chest tubes, tracheotomy, medicines given intravenously, and physical therapy kept him alive. In reality, God stood in the shadows, keeping watch over His own.

We prayed, checking texts for good news. Prayer warriors sent texts filled with encouragement. They even looked for updates at three in the morning. Thousands on Facebook prayed and waited.

Suddenly, after 77 days in ICU, Charlie began getting better. We cheered when tubes were pulled from his chest and kidney dialysis stopped. Intravenous lines came out day by day. When his tracheotomy was removed, we shouted hallelujahs.

We wept, viewing a video of Charlie finally seeing and holding his two-month-old daughter for the first time. And after more than three months in the hospital Charlie was released to go home.

Nearly a year later, Charlie is walking, driving a car, having daily physical therapy to improve walking, on nutrition regime and lifting weights. He still suffers from intense pain, but, month by month, we see improvements as he slowly recovers.

We witnessed a miracle! Words cannot express our gratitude for each of you who prayed. Great is thy faithfulness, oh, God our Father.

CPSIA information can be obtained
at www.ICGtesting.com
Printed in the USA
BVHW070321221022
649853BV00002B/3